DISCOVERING AMERICA

Mid-Atlantic

DELAWARE • MARYLAND • PENNSYLVANIA

By
Thomas G. Aylesworth
Virginia L. Aylesworth

CHELSEA HOUSE PUBLISHERS
New York • Philadelphia

3   5   7   9   8   6   4   2

Library of Congress Cataloging-in-Publication Data

Aylesworth, Thomas G.
   Mid-Atlantic: Delaware, Maryland, Pennsylvania
Thomas G. Aylesworth, Virginia L. Aylesworth.
    p. cm.—(Discovering America)
   Includes bibliographical references and index.
   ISBN 0-7910-3402-X.
     0-7910-3420-8 (pbk.)
    1. Middle Atlantic States—Juvenile literature. 2. Delaware—Juvenile literature. 3. Maryland—
Juvenile literature. 4. Pennsylvania—Juvenile literature. I. Aylesworth, Virginia L. II. Title.
III. Series: Aylesworth, Thomas G. Discovering America.

F106.A95   1995   94-43816
974—dc20   CIP
                                     AC

CONTENTS

PENNSYLVANIA

Delaware

The great seal of the state of Delaware was first designed in 1777, and has been only slightly changed since then. It is circular and in the center is a medal with a sheaf of wheat, an ear of corn, and an ox to represent the state's early farms. On the left side of the shield is a farmer, and on the right a rifleman, who stand for the people of Delaware as productive workers and defenders of their rights. Over the medal is a ship. Underneath the artwork is a scroll bearing the state motto. Around the circle are the words "Great Seal of the State of Delaware" and the dates 1793, 1847, and 1907. These dates were intended to signify the years in which the state seal was amended, but a mistake was made—"1907" should have been "1911."

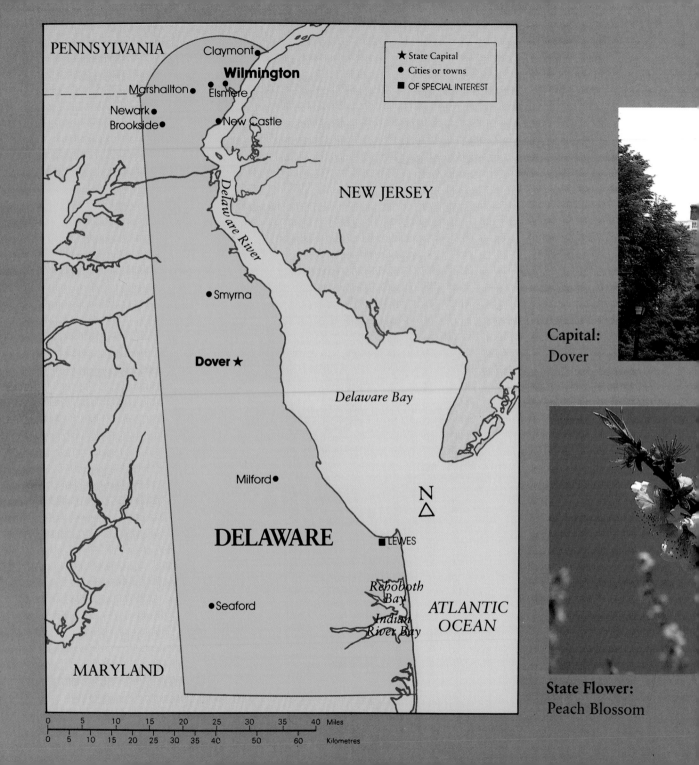

PENNSYLVANIA

Claymont

Wilmington

Marshallton •
Elsmere

Newark •
Brookside •

New Castle •

Delaware River

NEW JERSEY

• Smyrna

Dover ★

Delaware Bay

• Milford

N
△

DELAWARE

■ LEWES

Rehoboth Bay

ATLANTIC
OCEAN

Indian River Bay

• Seaford

MARYLAND

★ State Capital
● Cities or towns
■ OF SPECIAL INTEREST

0   5   10   15   20   25   30   35   40 Miles
0   5 10 15 20 25 30 35 40 45 50 55 60 Kilometres

Capital:
Dover

State Flower:
Peach Blossom

DELAWARE

At a Glance

State Flag

Major Industries:
Chemical research and manufacturing, agriculture, shellfishing, food processing

Major Crops:
Soybeans, potatoes, corn, wheat, apples

Size: 2,045 square miles (49th largest)
Population: 689,214 (46th largest)

State Bird:
Blue Hen Chicken

State Flag

The state flag of Delaware was adopted in 1913, and it contains an adaptation of the state seal. It is a colonial blue banner with a large buff diamond in the center. In the diamond is the artwork from the state seal with the state motto on a scroll beneath the figures. Underneath is the date, December 7, 1787, of Delaware's ratification of the Constitution.

State Motto

Liberty and Independence

This became the motto of the state in 1847, when it was added to the state seal, and it was a salute to the ideals of American government.

Autumn on Silver Lake in Delaware's capital.

State Name and Nicknames

In the beginning, the English explorers named the Delaware River after Sir Thomas West, Lord de la Warr, who had been appointed the first governor of the Virginia Colony. The Native Americans of the vicinity, the Lenapes, soon were called the Delaware Indians, and finally, the area became known as Delaware.

The most common nickname of the state is the *First State*, since it was the first to ratify the United States Constitution. But it is also referred to as the *Diamond State*, based upon a quotation from Thomas Jefferson, who said it was like a diamond—"small, but of great value."

State Flower

The peach blossom was adopted as the state flower by the state legislature in 1955, since it had been the official floral emblem since 1895. Public sympathy had leaned toward the goldenrod, but after agriculturalists and schoolchildren sent in many petitions to the legislature pointing out that there were more than 80,000 peach trees in the state, the blossom was accepted.

State Tree

Ilex opaca, the American holly, was selected as the state tree of Delaware in 1939. It is also called holly, white holly, evergreen holly, and boxwood.

State Fish

The weakfish, genus *Cynoscion*, was adopted in 1981.

State Mineral

Sillimanite was selected as the state mineral in 1975.

State Song

The state song of Delaware, "Our Delaware," was adopted in 1925. The lyricist was George B. Hynson and the composer was William M. S. Brown.

State Capital

New Castle was the capital of the Delaware Colony from 1704 to 1777, and then the government seat was moved to Dover.

State Bird

The blue hen chicken was named the state bird in 1939. The reason was that during the Revolutionary War, a company of soldiers from Delaware's Kent County would stage cockfights between blue hen chickens between battles. As a result, the group became known as the Blue Hen's Chickens, a name that reappeared during the Civil War.

State Beverage

The state beverage of Delaware is milk, and it was adopted in 1983.

State Insect

The ladybug, or ladybird, *Hippodamia convergens*, was named state insect in 1973.

Population

The population of Delaware in 1992 was 689,214, making it the 46th most populous state. There are 352.5 people per square mile—66.4 percent of them in metropolitan areas.

Agriculture

The chief crops of the state are soybeans, potatoes, corn, mushrooms, lima beans, green peas, barley, cucumbers, watermelons, apples, and snap beans. Delaware is also a livestock state, and there are estimated to be some 31,000 cattle, 39,000 hogs, and 236.5 million broilers on its farms. Construction sand and gravel, plus greensand marl, are important mineral products. Commercial fishing brought in $4.2 million in 1992.

Government

The governor is elected to a four-year term, as are the lieutenant governor, the attorney general, and the

Grain silos, found on farms throughout the state, are used for the storage of barley, one of the state's most important crops.

insurance commissioner. The state legislature, which meets every year, consists of a 21-member Senate elected to 4-year terms and a 41-member House of Representatives elected to 2-year terms. The present state constitution was adopted in 1897. In addition to its two U.S. senators, Delaware has one representative in the U.S. House of Representatives.

The state has three votes in the electoral college.

Industries

The principal industries of the state are chemical production, finance, auto assembly, food processing, and transportation equipment. The chief products are nylon, apparel, luggage, processed meats and vegetables, and railroad and aircraft equipment.

Sports

Many sporting events on the collegiate and secondary school levels are played throughout the state. Harness and thoroughbred racing are also popular, as is recreational fishing.

Major Cities

Dover (population 27,630). Settled in 1717, the state capital was laid out around its beautiful green by William Penn. Circling the green and on State Street are fine eighteenth- and nineteenth-century buildings. One of the major activities of the state government is the granting of charters to companies who want to take advantage of the state's corporation laws, which are extremely favorable. More than 60,000 United States firms are Delaware corporations.

Places to visit: the Delaware State Museum, the State House, the Hall of Records, the John Dickinson Plantation (1740), the Octagonal Schoolhouse (1836), the Island Field Archaeological Museum, and the Delaware Agricultural Museum.

Wilmington (population 71,529). Settled in 1631, Wilmington is the largest city in the state, and is sometimes called the "Chemical Capital of the World." The headquarters of E. I. du Pont de Nemours & Co. are here. The city turns out vulcanized fiber, glazed leathers, dyed cotton, rubber hose, autos, and many other products.

Places to visit: Holy Trinity (Old Swedes) Church (1698), Hendrickson House (1690), the Fort Christina Monument, the Grand Opera House (1871), the Old Town Hall (1798), Willingtown Square, the Delaware Art Museum, the Rockwood Museum, Brandywine Zoo and Park, Winterthur Museum and Gardens, the Hagley Museum, the Delaware Museum of Natural

The double-span Delaware Memorial Bridge, connects the state to New Jersey.

A charter boat sets out on a tour of the coast near Lewes.

History, the Nemours Mansion and Gardens, and the Greenbank Mill.

Places to Visit

The state of Delaware maintains 43 recreation areas.

Lewes: Restored buildings. This grouping includes the Cannon Ball House, the lightship *Overfalls*, the Coast Guard Boathouse (1890), the Thompson Country Store, Plank House, Rabbit's Ferry House, the Burton-Ingram House, the Ellegood House, and an old doctor's office.

New Castle: The Green. Originally laid out by the Dutch, this public square is surrounded by many historical buildings.

Odessa: Historic Houses of Odessa. Some of the old houses open to the public date back to the 1700s.

Smyrna: Historic buildings. Many public and private buildings are found here— built at the time when the town was called Duck Creek Village.

Events

There are many events and organizations that schedule activities of various kinds in the state of Delaware. Here are some of them.

Sports: Auto racing and harness racing at Dover Downs (Dover), horse racing at Brandywine Raceway (Wilmington), horse racing at Delaware Park (Wilmington).

Arts and Crafts: Spring Festival (Fenwick Island), Boardwalk Arts Festival (Fenwick Island), Delaware Nature Society Harvest and Craft Festival (Wilmington).

Music: Band concerts (New Castle), Bandstand concerts (Rehoboth Beach).

Entertainment: Coast Day (Lewes), Separation Day (New Castle), Indian Summer Festival (Rehoboth Beach), Old Fashioned Ice Cream Festival (Wilmington).

Tours: Old Dover Days (Dover), Dover Heritage Trail (Dover), Cottage Tour of Art (Rehoboth Beach), Wilmington Garden Day (Wilmington).

Rehoboth Beach, on Delaware's southern shore, is one of the state's principal summer resorts. Delaware's entire eastern border is coastline adjoining the Delaware River, Delaware Bay, and the Atlantic Ocean.

Bombay Hook, in Delaware's marshy mid-coast section, is actually an island nestling close to the shoreline. At the 17,000-acre Bombay Hook National Wildlife Refuge, more than 275 species of birds have been recorded.

The Land and the Climate

Delaware is smaller than any other state except Rhode Island. It occupies part of the Delmarva Peninsula and is bordered by New Jersey, the Delaware River, Delaware Bay, and the Atlantic Ocean on the east; Maryland on the south and west; and Pennsylvania on the north. Because it is so small, Delaware has only two land regions: the Atlantic Coastal Plain and the Piedmont.

Delaware

Sweet corn is sorted and packed on a farm near Dover. Fruits and vegetables make up about one-third of the state's cash farm income.

The Atlantic Coastal Plain comprises most of Delaware except for the northern tip of the state. It is part of the long strip that stretches along the Atlantic coast from New Jersey to southern Florida. In Delaware, the plain rarely rises more than 80 feet above sea level, and it includes a 30,000-acre swamp along the southern boundary of the state. The Atlantic Coastal Plain supports vast soybean fields that cover about half the state's cultivated land, as well as corn, hay, and wheat fields. Dairy, poultry, and vegetable farms (called truck farms) dot the level landscape, and orchards produce fruit for the market, including several kinds of apples. Along the coast, especially at the edge of Delaware Bay, fishing and the harvesting of shellfish contribute to Delaware's economy. The manufacturing plants of the Coastal Plain produce chemicals, leather goods, canned foods, and other products.

Above:
An enticing display of fresh Delaware produce. Sussex County, in the southern part of the state, is favored by farmers over northern areas for its longer growing season and richer soil.

At left:
A typical Delaware farm scene. Wheat, corn, fruits and vegetables, poultry, and fishing are the basis of the state's agricultural and food-processing industries.

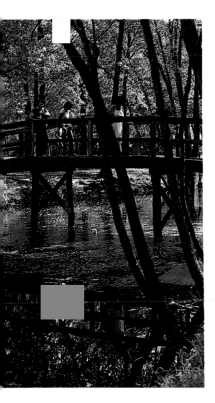

The Piedmont, part of a hilly region that extends from New Jersey to Alabama, crosses Delaware in the north. It forms a narrow strip that seldom exceeds 10 miles in width. The Piedmont is an area of fertile fields and low hills. It includes the highest point in the state (in New Castle County), which is only 442 feet above sea level. Large farms, especially dairy farms, and equally large estates are found here.

The coastline of Delaware extends only 28 miles from the Maryland border to the mouth of Delaware Bay. But if all the bays, creeks, rivers, and sounds are included, there are 381 miles of shoreline. The Delaware River is the state's largest and most important; with Delaware Bay, it makes the state an international shipping center. The most important of the smaller rivers are the Christina, Broadkill, Indian, Mispillion, Murderkill, Nanticoke, and St. Jones.

Temperatures vary little from one end of Delaware to the other. In January they average 36 degrees Fahrenheit, and in July, 76 degrees F. Rainfall, melted snow, and other forms of precipitation average 45 inches per year. Snowfall is slightly higher in the northern part of the state, but the Atlantic coast receives only about a foot of snow per winter.

Above:
Silver Lake is a peaceful spot in Dover. Many of the state's small lakes were made by damming creeks during colonial times to supply water power to saw and grist mills.

At right:
The Brandywine area, in northern Delaware, is typical of the state's flat, open land. The Brandywine Creek is the principal tributary of the Christina River, one of the state's important waterways.

The History

When the first white settlers arrived in what would become the state of Delaware, several Algonkian tribes were living there. Most important were the Lenni Lenape, along the banks of the Delaware River, who would later be known as the Delaware. Most of the Indians would be forced out of the territory by the mid-1770s.

The first Europeans to see the Delaware region were probably Henry Hudson and his crew. Hudson was an English sailor who had been employed by the Dutch East India Company to search for a route to the Far East. He sailed into what would be called Delaware Bay in 1609 and headed north up the Delaware River. The following year Captain Samuel Argall of the Virginia Colony sailed into the bay, seeking refuge from a storm. He named it De la Warr Bay for Lord de la Warr, the first governor of Virginia, who had commissioned the expedition. Two Dutch explorers, Cornelius Hendricksen and Cornelis Mey, visited the area in 1613–14.

Captain Peter Heyes led the first group of settlers to Delaware from Hoorn in the Netherlands. Their ship, *The Whale*, landed at Zwaanendael (Swan Valley) near the present city of Lewes in 1631. This was the first white settlement in the region, but a year later the town was destroyed and its inhabitants massacred by Indians. The 28 men of the Dutch party had had an argument with a Lenni Lenape chief, and the bones of all but one of the settlers were found, with those of their cattle, strewn over their burned fields.

Swedish settlers led by Peter Minuit, who had been dismissed as governor of New Netherland by the Dutch, arrived in 1638 near what is now Wilmington. They founded the colony of New Sweden and built Fort Christina, naming it for their young queen. The Swedish settlers built the first log cabins in America, and Minuit was appointed the first governor. Meanwhile, the Dutch government resented the presence of New Sweden in what it considered Dutch

Dutch explorer Peter Minuit led a party of settlers to Fort Christina (now Wilmington) in 1638. There they established the first permanent white settlement in what is now Delaware.

territory and set up a Swede-watching post called Fort Casimir (now New Castle). This was done by order of Peter Stuyvesant, governor of New Netherland, in 1651. The new Swedish governor, Johan Rising, captured Fort Casimir by surprise in 1654, but the following year Stuyvesant's troops recaptured it and took Fort Christina as well.

The Delaware region passed into British hands in 1664, along with the northern Dutch colony of New Netherland, renamed New York. The British governed the Delaware area as part of the New York colony. The Dutch recaptured the region in 1673, but returned it to the British without bloodshed the following year.

In 1682 William Penn came from England to found his Pennsylvania colony. He had acquired title to the Delaware region to give his holdings access to the Atlantic Ocean. Delaware became a territory of the Pennsylvania colony, known as the Three Lower Counties because it was south of Pennsylvania on the Delaware River. The Delaware territory had the same number of representatives to the Pennsylvania legislature as did the rest of the colony. But while Penn and Lord Baltimore, of the colony of Maryland, wrangled over whose lands were whose, the Lower Counties were left to defend themselves against sea-going privateers and land-based colonial warfare. As Pennsylvania added more counties, they also feared that they would soon have a minority voice in the colonial legislature. Thus the Three Lower Counties refused, in 1701, to meet with the other delegates. They asked William Penn to grant them a separate legislature, and he agreed. They set up their own legislature in 1704 and proclaimed Delaware's boundaries in 1775, based on the surveys of Mason and Dixon during the 1760s. Until the Revolutionary War, however, the Three Lower Counties continued to be ruled by the governor of Pennsylvania.

During the 1760s, George III of England began to impose severe taxes on the American colonies, and the resentful Three Lower Counties sent delegates to the First Continental Congress in Philadelphia in 1774. The Revolutionary War began the following year, and in 1776 came the momentous meeting of the Second Continental Congress and Caesar Rodney's famous ride, which may well have been more important to the United States than the ride of Paul Revere and his companions. The Declaration of Independence had been written and was up for approval. Rodney, a delegate to the Congress, was at home in Dover at the time. But on July 1, 1776, he made an 86-mile horseback run from Dover to Philadelphia to break a tie vote and enable Delaware to approve the Declaration of Independence, which was adopted the following day and officially proclaimed on July 4th. Later that year, Delaware became the Delaware State, adopting its first constitution and electing John

Fort Christina, in Wilmington, was built as a fur-trading and tobacco-exporting post by Peter Minuit and his party. The business venture was begun by a Swedish company financed partly by Dutch investors. Soon disappointed by the lack of profits, the Dutch withdrew and left the company to be reorganized under the Swedish government.

Above:
Guides in Old New Castle wear costumes of the 1700s. One of the state's most popular historic centers, New Castle is the site of Amstel House, the home of Delaware's seventh governor, Nicholas Van Dyke.

Above right:
The Old Court House in New Castle was constructed before 1732 on the town green. It was Delaware's capitol until 1777.

McKinly as its first president (governor). New Castle was designated the capital. The hard-riding Rodney served as the state's second governor, from 1778 to 1781.

Delaware sent a remarkable total of almost 4,000 men to the Revolutionary War, in which they were nicknamed "the Blue Hen's Chickens" for the gamecocks they brought along from their native state. (Delaware's Blue Hen Chicken would later be designated the state bird.) "The Delaware Line" was a crack regiment of the Continental Army. After heavy casualties in 1780, the unit was reorganized. Its men would "fight all day and dance all night," according to a dispatch by General Nathanael Greene.

The only Revolutionary War battle on Delaware soil was fought at Cooch's Bridge, near Newark, in 1777. The outnumbered Americans retreated, and the British went on to Pennsylvania, where they defeated General George Washington's forces in the Battle of Brandywine and occupied Wilmington the following day. Because of the closeness of British troops, the capital of Delaware was moved from New Castle to Dover.

On February 22, 1779, Delaware signed the Articles of Confederation, the forerunner to the United States Constitution. But when it came time to write the constitution, Delaware statesman John Dickinson, "the Penman of the Revolution," and one of the state's five delegates to the Constitutional Convention, was instrumental in the decision to write a new document rather than simply patching up the Articles of Confederation. With characteristic willingness to stand up and be counted, Delaware was the first of the original 13 states to ratify the Constitution—on December 7, 1787. In 1792 it adopted a new state constitution and changed its name from the Delaware State to the State of Delaware.

After the Revolution, Wilmington became the most important flour-milling city in the nation, and in 1802, Éleuthère Irénée du Pont established a powder mill on the banks of the Brandywine Creek near Wilmington. This was the beginning of the du Pont industrial empire and the great chemical plants and research facilities of the state. During the War of 1812, when the British captain Beresford fired on Lewes, its defenders, lacking ammunition, showed their resourcefulness by returning his fire with his own cannon balls—and sent him flying for Bermuda so fast that he forgot to take on fresh water.

Before the Civil War, Delaware was a slave state, but many of its people had strong ties with both Union and Confederacy when hostilities broke out in 1861. Delaware fought on the Union side, but many of its citizens thought that the Southern states should have been permitted to secede, or withdraw, from the Union peaceably. Delaware slaves were freed in 1865, with the 13th Amendment to the United States Constitution.

From the middle of the 19th century, the construction of railroads in Delaware helped farmers move their crops to the cities, and

Wilmington, the state's largest city, is the center of Delaware's manufacturing economy. During the early 19th century, when the state was growing quickly, many industries were attracted to the Wilmington area by its abundant water power.

Wilmington continued its growth as an industrial center. Thousands of people settled there to work in the shipyards, iron foundries, machine shops, and manufacturing plants.

The early 20th century saw major improvements in education, public welfare, and road building in the state. Delaware had long been aware of the importance of education. The University of Delaware was founded in 1743, and the first library in the region was established in Wilmington in 1754. Free public education had been mandatory since the late 18th century, and in the early 20th century, industrial magnate Pierre S. du Pont contributed several million dollars to education in Delaware.

The Great Depression of the 1930s put thousands of Delaware factory workers and farmers out of work along with millions of other Americans, but it prompted much-needed reforms in state government. The massive federal assistance projects initiated by Franklin D. Roosevelt's administration also helped Delaware to revive economically. By the time the United States entered World War II in 1941, the state's mills and factories were prepared to turn out materials needed by the armed forces. Wilmington's Dravo shipyards became the state's major employer.

After the war, Delaware's population began to increase dramatically—some 40 percent in the 1950s alone. One factor was Delaware's low corporate tax rates, and a state law that allows businesses to incorporate in Delaware even if they do most of their business outside the state. As a result, some 60,000 businesses have incorporated in this small "corporate capital of the world." Another factor in Delaware's postwar growth was completion of the Delaware Memorial Bridge, linking the state with New Jersey, in 1951. In 1971, the Coastal Zone Act was proposed prohibiting the development of new heavy industry along the Delaware coastline. In the early 1980s, Delaware had no state sales, real estate, or personal property taxes. This, in combination with its central location to New York and Washington, continued to attract out-of-state banks and corporations to Delaware. In the early 1990s, while most states were suf-

fering from a recession, Delaware's economy was booming and the state had a budget surplus. What the Bard of Milford, John Lofland, wrote of the state in 1847 is still true today: Delaware is "like a diamond, diminutive, but having within it inherent value."

The People

Delaware is an urban state, with over 66 percent of its residents living in metropolitan areas. About 96 percent of Delawareans were born in the United States, of the rest, most came from England, France, Germany, and Italy. The largest religious groups are the Roman Catholics and the Methodists. Other major denominations include the Baptists, Episcopalians, Lutherans, and Presbyterians.

Above left:
Dough for deep-frying is poured at the annual Greek Festival in Wilmington.

Above:
Bagpipes are tuned at the Irish Workers Festival. During the 1800s many Irish, Germans, Italians, and Poles settled in Delaware.

Below:
American naval officer Thomas Macdonough was born in New Castle County. During the War of 1812, he commanded the U.S. naval squadron on Lake Champlain.

John Marquand fought in France during World War I.

Famous People

Many famous people were born in the state of Delaware. Here are a few:

James Asheton Bayard 1799-1880, Wilmington. Senator from 1767-1815

Emily Perkins Bissell 1861-1948, Wilmington. Headed the first Christmas Seal drive to aid children with tuberculosis

Henry Sidell Canby 1878-1961, Wilmington. Editor, author, publisher, and educator. Co-founder of *The Saturday Review of Literature*

Annie J. Cannon 1863-1941, Dover. Astronomer

John Middleton Clayton 1796-1856, Dagsborough. Served 3 terms as a U.S. Senator from Delaware

Francis Irénée du Pont 1873-1942, Wilmington. Chemist who made basic discoveries in the field of smokeless gunpowder

Pierre du Pont 1870-1954, Wilmington. Chairman of E. I. du Pont de Nemours Chemical Company

Robert Fulton 1765-1815, Fulton. Inventor of the practical steamboat

Thomas MacDonough 1783-1825, MacDonough. Naval officer and commander in the War of 1812

John P. Marquand 1893-1960, Wilmington. Pulitzer Prize-winning novelist: *The Late George Apley*

Daniel Nathans b.1928, Wilmington. Nobel Prize-winning biologist

Howard Pyle 1853-1911, Wilmington. Author and illustrator of children's books: *The Merry Adventures of Robin Hood*

Caesar Rodney 1728-1784, Dover. President of Delaware and signer of the Declaration of Independence

Randy White b.1953, Wilmington. Football player

Colleges and Universities

There are only a few colleges and universities in Delaware. Here are the more prominent, with their locations, dates of founding, and enrollment.

Delaware State College, Dover, 1891, 2,935

Goldey-Beacom College, Wilmington, 1886, 1,757

University of Delaware, Newark, 1743, 17,489

Wesley College, Dover, 1873, 1,294

Wilmington College, New Castle, 1967, 2,500

Delaware Tourism Office
One Commerce Center
Wilmington, DE 19801
or call, 1-800-441-8846

Maryland

The seal of Maryland was first sent to the colony from England shortly after its settlement, and readopted in 1876. It is circular, and on one side has the figure of the Lord Proprietor in full armor on horseback. Surrounding the seal is the Latin inscription *Caecilius Absolutus Dominus Terrae Marieae et Avaloniae Baro de Baltimore* (Cecil Absolute Lord of Maryland and Avalon, Baron of Baltimore). Avalon refers to a settlement in Newfoundland that also had been sponsored by Lord Baltimore. On the reverse, the shield in the center carries the coats of arms of the Calvert and Crossland families, as combined by Lord Baltimore, who was related to both. On the left of the shield is a farmer, who represents Maryland. On the right is a fisherman, who represents Lord Baltimore's Avalon Colony in Newfoundland. Above the shield is an earl's coronet, and above that a helmet. At the bottom, on a scroll, is the motto, *Fatti Maschii Parole Femine*. In a circle around the seal is written *Scuto Bonae Voluntatis Tuae Coronasti Nos*, and the date 1632, the year the royal charter was granted.

MARYLAND
At a Glance

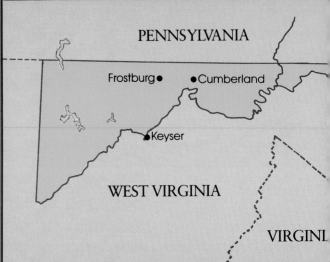

PENNSYLVANIA

Frostburg ● ● Cumberland

● Keyser

WEST VIRGINIA

VIRGINI

Major Crops:
Tobacco, corn, soybeans

Major Industries:
Metals, electronics, food products, fishing, tourism

Capital:
Annapolis

State Flower:
Black-eyed Susan

State Tree: White Oak

Nicknames: Old Line State, Free State

State Flag

State Bird:
Baltimore Oriole

Size: 10,460 sq. mi. (42nd largest)
Population: 4,908,453 (19th largest)

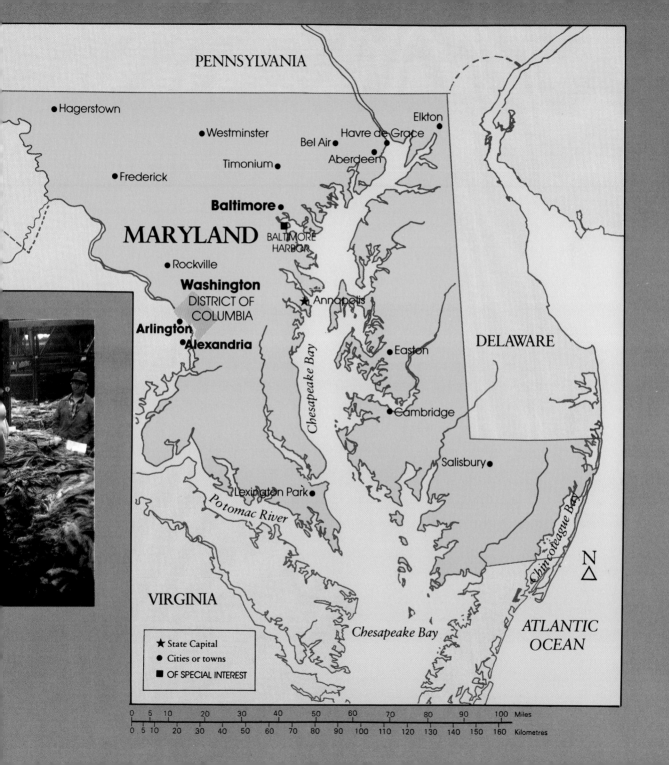

PENNSYLVANIA

● Hagerstown

● Westminster

Bel Air ●   Havre de Grace ●

● Frederick   Timonium ●   Aberdeen ●   Elkton ●

Baltimore ●

MARYLAND   ■ BALTIMORE HARBOR

● Rockville

Washington
DISTRICT OF
COLUMBIA   ★ Annapolis

Arlington ●
● **Alexandria**   DELAWARE

● Easton

Chesapeake Bay

● Cambridge

● Salisbury ●

Potomac River   ● Lexington Park ●   *Chincoteague Bay*

VIRGINIA

Chesapeake Bay   **ATLANTIC OCEAN**

N
△

★ State Capital
● Cities or towns
■ OF SPECIAL INTEREST

0 5 10   20   30   40   50   60   70   80   90   100 Miles
0 5 10   20   30   40   50   60   70   80   90 100 110 120 130 140 150 160 Kilometres

State Flag

The flag of Maryland was first flown in 1888 at the Gettysburg, Pa., battlefield, but it was not adopted officially until 1904. On it is the same coat of arms that was granted to Lord Baltimore—a combination of the Calvert and Crossland families' coats of arms.

State Mottos

Fatti Maschii Parole Femine

The first of the state's mottos is the motto of the Calvert family, whose members were so closely related to Maryland history, and means "Manly Deeds, Womanly Words" in Italian.

Scuto Bonae Voluntatis Tuae Coronasti Nos

The second motto means "With Favor Wilt Thou Compass Us As with a Shield" in Latin and comes from the twelfth verse of the Fifth Psalm in the Bible.

Valleys cutting through the Allegheny Mountains provided vital pathways to the early westward migrating settlers.

State Name and Nicknames

King Charles I of England granted a charter for the colony to Lord Baltimore with the provision that it be named Maryland in honor of the king's wife, Queen Henrietta Maria, who was usually called Queen Mary.

Maryland is called *The Old Line State*, and it may have been the idea of George Washington to praise the loyalty of Maryland's regular line troops who were so valuable in the Revolutionary War. It is also called the *Free State* on account of its refusal to pass an enforcement act for Prohibition in the 1920s.

State Flower

Rudbeckia hirta, the black-eyed susan, was made the state flower in 1918. It is also called the yellow daisy.

State Tree

The white oak, *Quercus alba*, was named the state tree in 1941.

State Bird

Naturally enough, the Baltimore oriole, *Icterus galbula*, is the state bird of Maryland, and was adopted in 1947. Lord Baltimore chose orange and black for the colors of his coat of arms because of his liking for the colors of this bird, which he often saw on his estate. Subsequently, the bird was named the Baltimore oriole.

State Boat

The skipjack, a sloop used by the Chesapeake Bay fishermen, was named the state boat in 1985.

State Capital

St. Mary's City was the capital of the state from 1634 to 1694, when Annapolis became the capital.

State Dog

The Chesapeake Bay retriever was an obvious choice as state dog in 1964.

State Fish

The striped bass, or rockfish, was chosen the state fish in 1965.

State Fossil Shell

Ecphora quadricostata, a primitive molusk related to the snail, was adopted as the state fossil shell in 1984.

State Insect

The Baltimore checkerspot butterfly, *Euphydryas phaeton*, naturally enough, was named state insect in 1973.

State Sport

The medieval sport of jousting, catching rings on a lance from a galloping horse, became the state sport in 1962. The State Jousting Championships are held at St. Margaret's near Baltimore every October.

State Summer Theater

The Olney Theatre in Montgomery County near Rockville was adopted as the state summer theater in 1978.

State Theater

Center Stage in Baltimore

was named the state theater in 1978.

State Song

"Maryland! My Maryland!" was adopted as the state song in 1939. The lyrics are a poem written in 1861 by James Ryder Randall, and the music is from the old German Christmas carol "O Tannenbaum," or "O Christmas Tree."

Population

The population of Maryland in 1992 was 4,908,453, and it is the 19th most populous state. There are 502.1 people per square mile—92.8 percent of them in metropolitan areas. About 94 percent of the people of Maryland were born in the United States.

Industries

The principal industry of the state is manufacturing. The chief products are electric and electronic equipment, food and similar products, and chemicals and allied products.

Agriculture

The chief crops of the state are tobacco, corn, and soybeans. Maryland is also a livestock state, and there are estimated to be some 315,000 cattle, 180,000 hogs and pigs, 33,000 sheep, 257.8 million poultry, and 280.5 million broilers on its farms. Hardwood timber is harvested, and crushed stone, sand, and gravel are important mineral resources. Commercial fishing earned $36.4 million in 1992.

Government

The governor is elected to a four-year term, as are the attorney general and the controller. The state legislature, called the general assembly, which meets annually, consists of a 47-member Senate and a 141-member House of Delegates. Both are elected to four-year terms. Each of the state's senatorial districts and each of Baltimore's six legislative districts elects one state senator. The delegate districts elect one to four delegates depending on population. The state's most recent constitution was adopted in 1867. In addition to its two U.S. senators, Maryland has eight representatives in the U.S. House of Representatives. It has ten votes in the electoral college.

USS Constellation

Maryland has the second highest percentage of people employed in construction (6.9%) in the United States, the third highest percentage of people employed in government jobs (23.5%), and the fourth highest percentage of people employed in the service sector (24.3%).

Sports

Many sporting events on the collegiate and secondary school levels are played in the state. In 1952, the University of Maryland won the Sugar Bowl. On the professional level, the Baltimore Orioles of the American League play baseball in their new stadium. Horse breeding and racing have long been important in Maryland. The Preakness is run every year at Pimlico, and there are many steeplechases as well.

Major Cities

Annapolis (population 33,195). Settled in 1649, Annapolis, the state capital, was planned and laid out as the provincial capital in 1695. It became the first peacetime capital of the United States when Congress met there from November 26, 1783, to August 13, 1784. The life of the town centers on state government business and the U.S. Naval Academy. Every May, at commencement time, thousands of visitors throng the narrow, historic streets.

Places to visit in Annapolis: The State House (1772-1779), the Old Treasury (1735), Government House (1868), McDowell Hall (1742-1789), Charles Carroll, Barrister House (1722), the Liberty Tree, the Hammond-Harwood House (1774), the Chase-Lloyd House (1769), the William Paca House and Garden, the Tobacco Prise House, the Revolutionary Soldiers Barracks, the Victualling Warehouse Maritime Museum, the United States Naval Academy, the London Town Publik House and Gardens (1760), and the Chesapeake Bay Bridge.

Baltimore (population 736,014). Settled in 1661, Baltimore is a major manufacturing center and a world seaport. It served as the nation's capital for more than two months during the Revolution and survived the Battle of Fort McHenry during the War of 1812.

Popular equestrian sports in Maryland range from traditional flat racing to steeplechase and jousting.

Recently, Baltimore has undergone a renaissance. Since the mid-1960s, the city has replaced hundreds of acres of slums, unused wharves, and rotting warehouses with new office and public buildings, parks, and museums.

Places to visit in Baltimore: The Washington Monument (1815-1842), the Walters Art Gallery, the Peabody Institute of the Johns Hopkins University, the Maryland Historical Society, Asbury House (1850), First Unitarian Church (1817), the Basilica of the Assumption of the Blessed Virgin Mary (1821), the Battle Monument (1815), City Hall, City Court House (1900), Lexington Market, the Peale Museum (1914), the Carroll Mansion (1811), the Shot Tower (1829), the Star-Spangled Banner Flag House and 1812 Museum, the Edgar Allan Poe House (1830), the Edgar Allan Poe grave, the Mother Seton House, the Fire Museum, Charles Center, the Jewish Heritage Center, the Holocaust Memorial, the National Aquarium,

Skipjacks, used for dredging oysters in Chesapeake Bay, are the last sail boats in commercial use in North America.

Harborplace, the Maryland Science Center, Top of the World, the U.S. frigate Constellation, the Baltimore Maritime Museum, the skipjack Minnie V., the Public Works Museum and Streetscape Sculpture, Federal Hill, the Old Otterbein United Methodist Church (1785-1786), Otterbein "Homesteading," Fort McHenry National Monument and Historic Shrine, the Baltimore Museum of Industry, the B & O Railroad Museum, the Babe Ruth Birthplace/ Baltimore Orioles Museum, the Mount Clare Mansion (1760), the H. L. Mencken House, the Baltimore Museum of Art, the Bufano Sculpture Garden, the Baltimore Zoo, the William Donald Schaefer Conservatory, the Cylburn Arboretum, Sherwood Gardens, the Baltimore Streetcar Museum, the

Cloisters Children's Museum, the Lovely Lane Museum, Fell's Point, City Fire Museum Engine Company #6, the Old Town Mall, Stirling Street "Homesteading," the Church Home and Hospital, and Patterson Park.

Places to Visit

The National Park Service maintains eight areas in the state of Maryland: Clara Barton National Historic Site, Antietam National Battlefield Site and Cemetery, Fort McHenry National Monument and Historic Shrine, Hampton National Historic Site, Assateague Island National Seashore, the Chesapeake and Ohio Canal National Historical Park, Cacoctin Mountain Park, and Fort Washington National Park. In addition, there are 39 state recreation areas.

Aberdeen: U.S. Army Ordnance Museum. On the Aberdeen Proving Grounds, there is a collection of tanks, self-propelled artillery, and ammunition, plus a weapons museum.

Boonsboro: Crystal Grottoes Caverns. Limestone caverns may be toured through a series of walkways.

College Park: NASA/ Goddard Visitor Center. This includes satellites, rockets, capsules, and exhibits on all fields of space research.

Cumberland: History House. Built about 1867, this is a restored 18-room residence.

Easton: Third Haven Friends Meeting House. This is one of the oldest frame-construction houses of worship in the country.

Ellicott City: B & O Railroad Station Museum. A model railroad presentation of the original track to Baltimore is a highlight of the displays in the restored station, the oldest in the United States (1830).

Emmitsburg: National Shrine Grotto of Lourdes. This is a one-third size replica of the famous French shrine to the Virgin Mary.

Frederick: Barbara Frietchie House and Museum. This was the home of the heroine of the nineteenth century poem by John

A maritime museum, science center and numerous shops and restaurants are located around Baltimore's harbor.

Greenleaf Whittier, Barbara Frietchie.

La Plata: Port Tobacco. Many old buildings are found on this site of one of the oldest continuously inhabited English settlements in North America.

Leonardtown: Sotterley. This working plantation was founded about 1717.

Rockville: Beall-Dawson House. This fine Federalist house was built in 1815.

St. Mary's City: Historic St. Mary's City. This outdoor museum contains several reconstructed seventeenth-century buildings, as well as a replica of the ship *Maryland Dove.*

St. Michaels: Chesapeake Bay Maritime Museum. This waterside museum explains the importance of the Bay in Maryland history with working exhibits, ship models and workboats.

Salisbury: Poplar Hill Mansion. Built about 1810, this is an excellent example of Georgian and Federal-style architecture.

Waldorf: John Wilkes Booth Escape Route. A tour of the places to which Booth fled after shooting Abraham Lincoln, including the Surratt House and Tavern (1852) in Clinton and the Dr. Samuel A. Mudd House (about 1830) in Ste. Catherine, begins here.

Events

There are many events and organizations that schedule activities of various kinds in the state of Maryland. Here are some of them.

Sports: Maryland Kite Festival (Baltimore), Baltimore International Jumping Classic (Baltimore), Horse racing at Pimlico Race Course (Baltimore), Sailboat Regatta (Cambridge), Jousting Tournament (Easton), Barbara Fritchie Motorcycle Races (Frederick), Horse racing at Laurel Race Course (Laurel), Winterfest (Oakland), $45,000 White Marlin Open (Ocean City), White Marlin Tournament (Ocean City), Harness racing at Delmarva Downs (Ocean City), Fishing Contests and Tournaments (Ocean City).

Arts and Crafts: Annapolis Arts Festival (Annapolis), Atlantic Crafts Council Crafts Fair (Baltimore), Maryland Arms Collectors Association Annual Antique Gun Show (Baltimore), Flower Mart (Baltimore), Frederick Craft Fair (Frederick), Lotus Blossom Festival (Frederick), Fall Festival (Frederick), National Craft Fair (Gaithersburg), Penn Alps Summerfest and Quilt Show (Grantsville), Frontier Craft Day (Hagerstown).

Music: Baltimore Opera Company (Baltimore), Baltimore Symphony (Baltimore), Harborlights Music Festival (Baltimore), the Pier 6 Concert Pavilion (Baltimore), Springs Folk Festival (Grantsville).

Entertainment: Maryland Renaissance Festival (Annapolis), Maryland Seafood Festival (Annapolis), U.S. Sailboat Show (Annapolis), U.S. Powerboat Show (Annapolis), Chesapeake Appreciation Day (Annapolis), Christmas in Annapolis (Annapolis), Chinese Lunar New Year Festival (Baltimore), Preakness Festival Week (Baltimore), Harbor Expo (Baltimore), Baltimore City Fair (Baltimore), New Year's Eve Extravaganza (Baltimore), Showcase of Nations Festival (Baltimore), Heritage Day (Bowie), Outdoor Show (Cambridge), Antique Aircraft Fly-In (Cambridge), Dorchester Seafood Feast-i-val (Cambridge), National Hard Crab Derby and Fair (Crisfield), Agricultural Expo and Fair (Cumberland), C & O Canal Boat Festival (Cumberland), Street Rod

Roundup (Cumberland), Seafood Festival (Cumberland), Tuckahoe Steam and Gas Show and Reunion (Easton), Waterfowl Festival (Easton), Sheep and Wool Festival (Ellicott City), Howard County Fair (Ellicott City), Treasury of Trains Show (Ellicott City), Christmas Garden Show (Ellicott City), Koi Festival (Frederick), Great Frederick Fair (Frederick), New Market Days (Frederick), Montgomery County Fair (Gaithersburg), Springs Folk Festival (Grantsville), Halfway Park Days (Hagerstown), Leitersburg Peach Festival (Hagerstown), Williamsport C & O Canal Days (Hagerstown), Smithsburg Steam and Craft Show (Hagerstown), Alsatia Mummers Halloween Parade Festival (Hagerstown), Fall Harvest Festival (Havre de Grace), Charles County Fair (La Plata), Blessing of the Fleet (Leonardtown), Saint Mary's County Fair (Leonardstown), Saint Mary's County Seafood Festival (Leonardstown), Garrett County Horse Shows (Oakland), Garrett County Fair (Oakland), Scottish Festival (Rockville), City of Rockville Day (Rockville), Antique Car Show (Rockville), Grand Militia Muster/Charter Days (St Mary's City), Maritime Heritage Festival (St Mary's City), Maple Syrup (Thurmont), Spring Celebration (Thurmont), State Fair (Towson), John Hanson Patriots Fife and Drum Corps Muster (Waldorf), Civil War Encampment (Waldorf), Charles County Trade Fair and Home Show (Waldorf), Old-Fashioned Corn Roast Festival (Westminster).

Tours: Philadelphia Electric Company (Aberdeen), Historic Annapolis (Annapolis), Maryland House and Garden Pilgrimage (Baltimore), Catoctin Mountains Colorfest (Thurmont), John Wilkes Booth Escape Route Tour (Waldorf).

Theater: Annapolis Summer Garden Theatre (Annapolis), Cockpit in Court Summer Theatre (Baltimore), the Vagabond Players (Baltimore), the Morris Mechanic Theater (Baltimore), Olney Theatre (Olney).

The seafood of Maryland's Chesapeake Bay is celebrated at many local fairs and festivals.

Colleges and Universities

There are many colleges and universities in Maryland. Here are the more prominent, with their locations, dates of founding, and enrollment.

Bowie State University, Bowie, 1865, 4,437

College of Notre Dame of Maryland, Baltimore, 1848, 1,019

Columbia Union College, Tackoma Park, 1904, 1,121

Coppin State College, Baltimore, 1900, 2,816

Frostburg State University, Frostburg, 1898, 5,295

Goucher College, Towson, 1885, 883

Hood College, Frederick, 1893, 2,005

Johns Hopkins University, Baltimore, 1876, 4,613

Loyola College, Baltimore, 1852, 6,221

Morgan State University, Baltimore, 1867, 5,307

Mount Saint Mary's College, Emmitsburg, 1808, 1,723

St. John's College, Annapolis,

The U.S. Naval Academy in Annapolis attracts many visitors who come to see the campus and the uniformed students.

1696, 408

Salisbury State University, Salisbury, 1925, 6,022

Towson State University, Towson, 1866, 15,232

United States Naval Academy, Annapolis, 1845, 4,265

University of Maryland at Baltimore, Baltimore, 1807, 3,101, *Baltimore County,*

Baltimore, 1963, 10,654; *College Park,* College Park, 1856, 32,858; *Eastern Shore,* Princess Anne, 1886, 2,430; *University College,* College Park, 1947, 38,567

Washington College, Chestertown, 1782, 886

Western Maryland College, Westminster, 1867, 2,143

Tobacco growing on a farm in southern Maryland. One of Maryland's major crops, it is grown primarily in the southwestern part of the state.

The Land and the Climate

Maryland prides itself on its variety of terrain. Green mountains in the western counties contrast with white Atlantic beaches. Chesapeake Bay, running northeast to south, divides the state into the Western Shore and the Eastern Shore and gives Maryland many of its excellent harbors. Western Maryland is a district of hills, mountains, valleys, and plateaus; the eastern section is relatively low and flat. The highest point in this state that borders Pennsylvania, Delaware, Virginia, and West Virginia is Backbone Mountain, which rises 3,360 feet above sea level. Maryland has five main land areas.

They are, from east to west: the Atlantic Coastal Plain, the Piedmont, the Blue Ridge, the Appalachian Ridge and Valley, and the Appalachian Plateau.

The Atlantic Coastal Plain, which runs along the east coast of the United States from New Jersey to southern Florida, covers the entire Eastern Shore and part of the Western Shore. It begins in the northeastern tip of Maryland and widens across a large portion of southern Maryland, extending almost to Washington, D.C. The area is flat on the Eastern Shore, but rises to 400 feet in some parts of the Western Shore. The region includes not only the major port city of Baltimore, but also a vast rural area with tobacco farms that have existed since colonial times; soybean, corn, rye, and poultry farms; fruit orchards; and the vast area of Chesapeake Bay, with its crab, clam, and oyster harvest. Clay, sand, and gravel beds are also found here.

The Piedmont, which stretches from New Jersey to Alabama, is about 50 miles wide as it extends through Maryland just west of the Atlantic Coastal Plain. It is characterized by low hills and fertile valleys, in which the most important agricultural activity is dairy farming.

The Blue Ridge, which extends from southern Pennsylvania to northern Georgia, is, in Maryland, a narrow, mountainous strip just west of the Piedmont. Most of the region is higher than 1,000 feet above sea level.

West of the Blue Ridge is the Appalachian Ridge and Valley Region, which stretches southwestward from New Jersey to Alabama. In Maryland, this strip separates Pennsylvania from West Virginia. The eastern part of the region, the Great Valley, is known in Maryland as Hagerstown Valley and is filled with orchards and farms. The western part of the area is covered with forests.

The Appalachian Plateau, which runs from New York to Georgia, is triangle-shaped in western Maryland; the Allegheny Mountains (spelled "Alleghany" in Maryland) extend through the region. Most of the area is heavily wooded.

Chestertown is in Kent County, on the northeastern side of Chesapeake Bay, where fishing is one of the primary industries. The bay yields a great variety of fish and shellfish, including crabs, oysters, clams, bluefish, flounder, shad, pike, bass, sea trout, and perch.

The Atlantic coastline of Maryland is a mere 31 miles long, but the countless arms and inlets of Chesapeake Bay give the state a total coastline of 3,190 miles. The Eastern Shore contains seven large rivers—the Chester, Choptank, Elk, Nanticoke, Pocomoke, Sassafras, and Wicomico. The Western Shore has the Gunpowder, Patapsco, and Patuxent Rivers, all of which flow into Chesapeake Bay. The Susquehanna River descends from Pennsylvania and empties into Chesapeake Bay, and the Potomac forms the state's southern and southwestern boundary.

Maryland's summers are hot (July temperatures average around 76 degrees Fahrenheit) and its winters are generally mild (temperatures range from 25 to 44 degrees F. in January). The climate is relatively humid, although much less so at the shore. Precipitation averages about 43 inches per year.

The History

Before European explorers came to what is now Maryland, Indians had been living in the area for hundreds of years. Most of them were Algonkians, but there were a few Susquehannock as well. The Algonkian tribes were the Choptank, Nanticoke, Piscataway, and others. Most of them moved into other states as the Europeans, and later the Americans, settled near or on their lands.

The Spaniards were the first to visit what is now Maryland. They explored Chesapeake Bay in the 1500s, but did not stay. In 1608 Captain John Smith of the Virginia colony sailed north up Chesapeake Bay into the Maryland region and wrote a description of his findings, but he established no settlements. In 1631 William Claiborne, also of Virginia, opened a trading post on Kent Island in the bay—the first white settlement in the territory.

Maryland's three and a half centuries of history really began, however, in March 1634. In 1632 Charles I of England had granted the Maryland region to George Calvert, the first Lord Baltimore, but Calvert died before the king could sign the charter. Charles then granted the area to Calvert's son Cecil, the second Lord Baltimore, and it was named Maryland for Charles's wife, Queen Henrietta Maria. So it was that in 1634 a pair of small ships, the *Ark* and the *Dove*, dropped anchor just above the mouth of the Potomac River. The settlers were led by Leonard Calvert, the brother of Cecil, who knelt solemnly on St. Clements Island (now Blakiston Island) and claimed his new province as Maryland. The ships then carried the 222 settlers, including religious refugees, to an Indian village near the southern tip of the Western Shore, which they purchased and renamed St. Mary's City. This village became, in a manner of speaking, the capital of a sort of private country, of which the Calvert family were sole owners.

Although their power in Maryland was absolute, the Calverts must have seemed alarmingly liberal to their 17th-century contemporaries. From the beginning, the settlers were allowed to elect their own governor (Leonard Calvert was the first). The Calverts themselves were Roman Catholics, but people of all religions were welcomed into the colony. The colonists were encouraged to suggest laws and to assist the governor in the performance of his duties. In 1649 religious toleration was guaranteed by law in Maryland, and a group of Puritans fled Virginia to settle there. But William Claiborne, whose settlement on Kent Island was part of Maryland, refused to recognize the authority of the Calverts and organized a group of Protestants who overthrew the government.

The English government stepped in in 1658 and ordered Claiborne to return the colony to Lord Baltimore. And the Calverts promised again to uphold the religious toleration act of 1649. But many Protestants resented Roman Catholic ownership of the colony, and in 1689 the Protestant Association, led by John Coode, seized control. Coode demanded that England take over the region and depose the Calverts, and in 1691 royal governors appointed by the king began to rule Maryland. In 1694 the capital was moved to Annapolis.

The Calvert family regained control of Maryland in 1715 under the fourth Lord Baltimore, who was a Protestant. The colony would remain in the family's hands until the Revolutionary War. In 1729, after two previous unsuccessful tries, the city of Baltimore was founded and became the colony's shipping and shipbuilding center. During this period many colonists grew wealthy from their tobacco crops and built mansions that are still standing today. In the middle 1700s, Maryland and Pennsylvania quarreled over the boundary line between the two colonies, and in 1763 they agreed to have Charles Mason and Jeremiah Dixon of England survey the land. The survey was completed in 1767, and the Maryland-Pennsylvania border became known as Mason and Dixon's Line.

Oppressive taxes and trade restrictions imposed by the British government in the mid-1700s aroused resentment in Maryland and the other colonies, which resisted them. The people of Maryland joined in protesting the Boston Port Bill—an attempt by King George III to punish the people of Boston for the Boston Tea Party of 1773. In 1774 Marylanders burned the British ship *Peggy Stewart* and its cargo of tea in Annapolis Harbor. Delegates from Maryland attended the First Continental Congress in Philadelphia in 1774 and supported a policy prohibiting the colonies from trading with England.

The Revolutionary War began in Massachusetts in April 1775. The following month the Second Continental Congress began its deliberations in Philadelphia, which resulted in the Declaration of Independence of July 1776. Charles Carroll of Carrollton was the best known of the four Maryland men who signed the declaration, but his fellow colonists were reluctant to relinquish their long-held powers to the Continental Congress. In December 1776 the Continental Congress moved to Baltimore because the British were threatening Philadelphia.

George Washington used this small cabin in Cumberland as one of his headquarters during the colonial wars. Armies were trained here for combat against the French and the Indians.

This elegant Georgian mansion, built in 1765, was the home of jurist William Paca, a signer of the Declaration of Independence. Paca was also a prominent member of the Maryland legislature and of the Continental Congress between 1768 and 1779.

Maryland had already been the scene of military action during the colonial wars. Indeed, the British general Edward Braddock, assisted by Colonel George Washington, had trained his army at Cumberland for the fight against the French and the Indians. And the bravery of Maryland troops in the Revolutionary War, as at the Battle of Long Island, won the state its nickname, "The Old Line State," for the strength of the Maryland line. British troops sailed into Chesapeake Bay in 1777 and landed at the mouth of the Elk River, whence they moved into Pennsylvania and defeated General Washington at the Battle of Brandywine. Maryland troops fought throughout the Revolution, and Baltimore industries built ships and cannons for the colonial forces.

During the war, the Continental Congress formed a government of the United States under the Articles of Confederation. But Maryland refused to sign the articles until 1781, when a dispute over the western boundaries of several states was resolved. After the war the Continental Congress met in Annapolis, at Maryland's invitation, and ratified the treaty with Britain that officially ended the Revolution and recognized the United States as an independent power. It was in the Maryland State House that George Washington resigned his commission as commander in chief of the Continental Army. Maryland ratified the new United States Constitution on April 28, 1788, and became the seventh state of the Union. Then, in 1791, Maryland gave land to Congress for the District of Columbia, the new national capital.

The War of 1812 is remembered in Maryland for the bombardment of Fort McHenry in Baltimore Harbor in September 1814. The British never did capture Baltimore, although they had burned the Capitol in Washington, D.C., a month earlier. During the Battle of Baltimore, Francis Scott Key, a lawyer from Frederick who was interned on a British ship in the harbor, composed "The Star-Spangled Banner," presumably "by the dawn's early light." It became the national anthem in 1931.

Other battles were fought in Maryland during the War of 1812.

During the War of 1812, it was here at Fort McHenry that British troops failed in a key attempt to take control of the Baltimore area. The British landed in Maryland in 1814, defeated American forces at Bladensburg, and proceeded to burn Washington, D.C., before their advance was thwarted at Fort McHenry. During the bombardment, Francis Scott Key wrote "The Star-Spangled Banner."

The British raided a number of towns and farmhouses along Chesapeake Bay in 1813. And in 1814 a British force under General Robert Ross sailed up the Patuxent River and defeated American forces in the Battle of Bladensburg.

Baltimore became a leading seaport during the early 1800s, and the opening of the Baltimore and Ohio Railroad in 1830 made the city the nation's first railroad center. In 1844 the world's first

The bloodiest battle of the Civil War was fought at Antietam on September 17, 1862. More than 22,000 casualties were counted that day, of whom 2,200 fell in just 20 minutes. Marylanders fought on opposing sides during the clash, which was the only major Civil War engagement fought on Maryland soil.

telegraphic message, "What hath God wrought?," was sent by inventor Samuel F. B. Morse from Washington, D.C., to Baltimore. And two major waterways linked Baltimore to western markets: the Chesapeake and Ohio Canal and the Chesapeake and Delaware Canal.

Although Maryland was a slave state, its people were divided in their loyalties between the Union and the Confederacy during the

Civil War. When Virginia seceded, or withdrew from the Union, federal troops rushed across Maryland to defend Washington, D.C., lest it become surrounded by Confederate states should Maryland secede. Maryland stayed with the Union, but many of its men joined the Confederate forces.

In 1862 General Robert E. Lee's Confederate army invaded Maryland, resulting in one of the bloodiest battles of the Civil War. The Battle of Antietam was fought near Sharpsburg on September 17. By the end of the day, some 12,000 Union soldiers and about 10,000 Confederates had been killed or wounded. Lee withdrew to Virginia, but in June of 1863 he marched across Maryland to Pennsylvania, where he lost the Battle of Gettysburg. In 1864 Confederate troops under General Jubal A. Early crossed the Potomac into Maryland and won the Battle of Monocacy, near Frederick. Maryland abolished slavery in 1864.

After the Civil War, Maryland's commercial and industrial development continued. Its location on Chesapeake Bay gave it close economic ties with the industrial Northeast, rather than the agricultural South. The state's factories and shipyards expanded mightily after the United States entered World War I in 1917. That year, the U.S. Army established its first testing center, the Aberdeen Proving Ground, on the shores of Chesapeake Bay.

The Great Depression of the 1930s was particularly hard on Baltimore, because the city was so industrialized. Maryland cooperated closely with the federal government in passing social and welfare legislation to promote economic recovery. When the United States entered World War II in 1941, Maryland's factories and shipyards began to produce airplanes, arms, warships, and other military equipment. Maryland farmers were called upon to contribute large quantities of food to the war effort.

After the war, Maryland enjoyed an economic boom that attracted many new people into the state. The Chesapeake Bay Bridge opened in 1952, connecting the Eastern and Western Shores. New airports, highways and tunnels forged closer links with surrounding communities. So many people have moved into the area, particularly around Baltimore and Washington, D.C., that experts predict that these two cities and their suburbs will become a single huge metropolitan area in the foreseeable future.

Education

Education in Maryland has a long history. The colony first provided funds for public education in 1694. Maryland's first free school was founded in 1696—King William's School in Annapolis, which is now the innovative St. John's College. Maryland provided for the establishment of public schools throughout the state in 1826. The sprawling University of Maryland was founded in 1807, and the prestigious Johns Hopkins University (famous for its fine medical school) was established in 1876. The United States Naval Academy was founded at Annapolis in 1845. The first libraries in Maryland were set up in 1699, and today the Enoch Pratt Free Library of Baltimore (founded in 1882) is one of the outstanding libraries in the nation.

The People

About 93 percent of Marylanders live in metropolitan areas. Some 94 percent of the residents of Maryland were born in the United States. The largest single religious group in the state is Roman Catholic, followed by Methodists, Baptists, Episcopalians, Jews, Lutherans, and Presbyterians.

Famous People

Many famous people were born in the state of Maryland. Here are a few:

Larry Adler b.1914, Baltimore. Classical harmonica player

Louis Bamberger 1855-1944, Baltimore. Founder of Bamberger and Co. department stores

Benjamin Banneker 1731-1806, Ellicott's Mills. Astronomer and surveyor

John Barth b.1930,

Frederick Douglass, born into slavery, escaped to New York in 1838, disguised as a sailor.

Dashiell Hammett's novel, The Maltese Falcon, *was made into a movie starring Humphrey Bogart.*

Cambridge. Novelist: *The Sot-Weed Factor*

Edwin Booth 1833-1893, Bel Air. Shakespearean actor

John Wilkes Booth 1838-1865, Bel Air. Actor and assassin of Abraham Lincoln

David K. E. Bruce 1898-1977, Baltimore. United States ambassador to France, West Germany, and Great Britain

William J. Burns 1861-1931, Baltimore. Founder of detective agency, later director of Bureau of Investigation (now FBI)

Francis X. Bushman 1883-1966, Baltimore. Movie actor: *Ben Hur*

James M. Cain 1892-1977, Annapolis: Novelist:*The Postman Always Rings Twice*

The legendary singer Billie Holiday had no formal musical education.

Baltimore native Thurgood Marshall dedicated much of his law practice to civil rights cases for the National Association for the Advancement of Colored People (NAACP). He became the first black associate justice of the U.S. Supreme Court in 1967 after serving for two years as solicitor general.

Charles Carroll 1737-1832, Annapolis. Revolutionary War leader and signer of the Declaration of Independence

John Carroll 1735-1815, Upper Marlboro. First U.S. Roman Catholic Bishop and founder of Georgetown University

Samuel Chase 1741-1811, Somerset County. Signer of the Declaration of Independence and Supreme Court justice

Stephen Decatur 1779-1820, Sinepuxent. Naval commodore in the Barbary Wars and the War of 1812

John Dickinson 1732-1808, Talbot County. Member of the Constitutional Convention

Frederick Douglass 1817-

Babe Ruth hit an astonishing 714 home runs in his baseball career.

Abolitionist Harriet Tubman was born a slave in Dorchester County. In 1847 she escaped to Pennsylvania, where she was befriended by a group of Quakers. Tubman soon became famous for her work with the Underground Railroad, which led hundreds of slaves to freedom in the North and Canada. After serving as a scout in the Union Army, she commanded 300 troops in a highly successful thrust into Confederate territory, where she freed more than 800 slaves. She remains the only American woman to have led a military action.

1895, Tuckahoe.
Abolitionist and orator
Cass Elliott 1941-1974,
Baltimore. Pop singer with
the Mamas and the Papas
Jimmie Foxx 1907-1967,
Sudlersville. Hall of Fame
baseball player
Lefty Grove 1900-1975,
Lonaconing. Hall of Fame
baseball pitcher
Dashiell Hammett 1894-
1961, Saint Mary's County.
Mystery novelist: *The
Maltese Falcon*
Matthew Henson 1866-1955,
Charles County.
Accompanied Robert
Peary to the North Pole in
1909
Billie Holiday 1915-1959,
Baltimore. Jazz/blues
singer
Johns Hopkins 1795-1873,
Anne Arundel County.
Developer and director of
the Baltimore and Ohio
Railroad
Al Kaline b.1934, Baltimore.
Hall of Fame baseball player
Francis Scott Key 1779-1843,
Carroll County. Attorney

and poet: "The Star-
Spangled Banner"
Bowie Kuhn b.1926, Tacoma
Park. Former
commissioner of baseball
Thurgood Marshall 1908-93,
Baltimore. Supreme Court
Justice
H. L. Mencken 1880-1956,
Baltimore. Critic: *American
Language*
Charles Wilson Peale 1741-
1827, Queen Anne's
County. Portrait painter
Emily Post 1873-1960,
Baltimore. Columnist and
writer: *Etiquette*
Francis P. Rous 1879-1970,
Baltimore. Nobel Prize-
winning physician
George Herman "Babe" Ruth
1895-1948, Baltimore. Hall
of Fame baseball player
Karl Shapiro b.1913,
Baltimore. Pulitzer Prize-
winning poet: *V-Letter and
Other Poems*
Pam Shriver b.1962,
Baltimore. Champion
tennis player
Upton Sinclair 1878-1968,
Baltimore. Pulitzer Prize-

winning novelist: *Dragon's
Teeth*
Raymond Spruance 1886-
1969, Baltimore. World
War II admiral
Henrietta Szold 1860-1945,
Baltimore. Zionist leader
and founder of Hadassah
Roger B. Taney 1777-1864,
Calvert County. Chief
Justice of the Supreme
Court
Harriet Tubman 1820-1913,
Dorchester County.
Abolitionist and leader of
the underground railroad
Leon Uris b.1924, Baltimore.
Novelist: *Exodus*
Chick Webb 1909-1939,
Baltimore. Drummer and
band leader
Frank Zappa 1940-94,
Baltimore. Rock Singer

**Where To Get More
Information**
Maryland Department of
Economic & Employment
Development
217 East Redwood Street
Baltimore, MD 21202
(410) 333-6970
or, 1-800-543-1036

Pennsylvania

Caleb Lownes of Philadelphia designed the Pennsylvania state seal in 1776 and it was approved in 1791. Slightly modified, it was re-approved in 1893. It is circular and, on a shield in the center are a ship (representing commerce, from the crest of Pennsylvania County), a plow (representing farming, from the crest of Chester County), and three sheaves of wheat (representing agricultural abundance, from the crest of Sussex County, which is now Delaware). Above the shield is an eagle, representing speed, strength, bravery, and wisdom. To the left of the shield is a stalk of corn, standing for plenty, and to the right is an olive branch, standing for peace. In a circle around the seal is written Seal of the State of Pennsylvania.

Capital: Harrisburg

State Flag

Major Industries:
Steel, machinery, minerals, agriculture, livestock

Major Crops:
Corn, hay, apples, vegetables, wheat

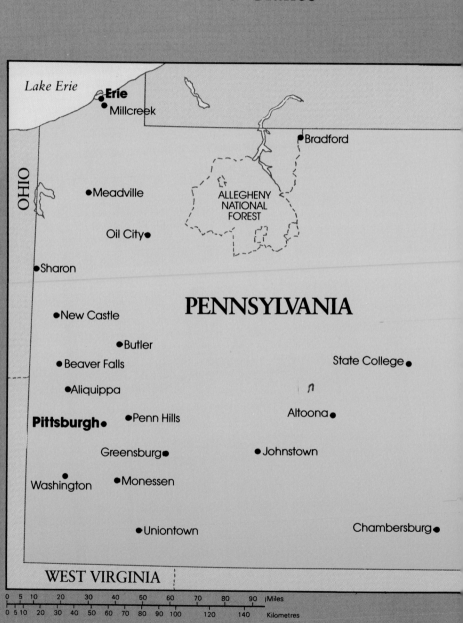

PENNSYLVANIA
At a Glance

Lake Erie

Erie
Millcreek

Bradford

OHIO

Meadville

ALLEGHENY NATIONAL FOREST

Oil City

Sharon

PENNSYLVANIA

New Castle

Butler

Beaver Falls

State College

Aliquippa

Pittsburgh Penn Hills

Altoona

Greensburg

Johnstown

Washington

Monessen

Uniontown

Chambersburg

WEST VIRGINIA

| 0 | 5 | 10 | 20 | 30 | 40 | 50 | 60 | 70 | 80 | 90 | Miles |

| 0 | 5 | 10 | 20 | 30 | 40 | 50 | 60 | 70 | 80 | 90 | 100 | 120 | 140 | Kilometres |

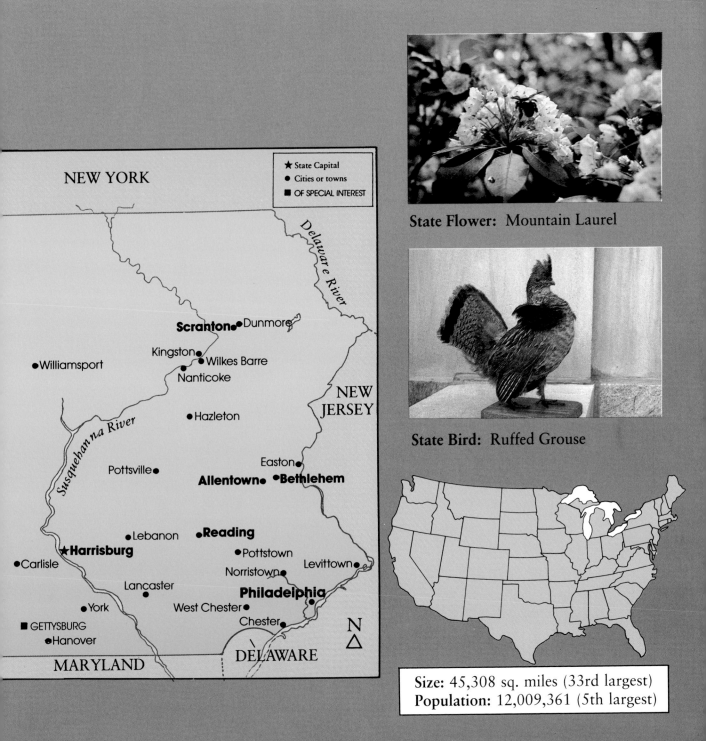

NEW YORK

★ State Capital
● Cities or towns
■ OF SPECIAL INTEREST

Delaware River

●Williamsport

Scranton●●Dunmore

Kingston●
●Wilkes Barre
Nanticoke

●Hazleton

NEW JERSEY

Susquehanna River

Pottsville●

Easton●

Allentown● ●Bethlehem

●Lebanon
●Reading

★Harrisburg
●Pottstown
●Carlisle
Levittown●
Norristown●
Lancaster
Philadelphia

●York
West Chester●
Chester●

■ GETTYSBURG
●Hanover

N
△

MARYLAND

DELAWARE

State Flower: Mountain Laurel

State Bird: Ruffed Grouse

Size: 45,308 sq. miles (33rd largest)
Population: 12,009,361 (5th largest)

State Flag

The flag of Pennsylvania was adopted in 1907. It is blue, with the shield from the state seal in the center, supported by two horses. Underneath, on a scroll, is the state motto.

State Motto

Virtue, Liberty, and Independence
When the state seal was designed, it included this motto, but it was not officially adopted until 1875.

The Pocono Mountains near the Delaware border are a popular year-round vacation spot.

State Capital

Harrisburg became the capital of Pennsylvania in 1812. But before that, the capitals were Chester (1681-1683), Philadelphia (1683-1799), and Lancaster (1799-1812).

State Name and Nicknames

Pennsylvania was named by King Charles II of England, who gave a charter to the area to William Penn in 1680. *Sylvania* in Latin means woods or woodland, and therefore Pennsylvania means "Penn's woods."

Pennsylvania is most commonly nicknamed the *Keystone State*, probably because it was located in the center of the original 13 colonies. It is also referred to as the *Quaker State* because Penn and his followers were members of the Society of Friends, a religious organization whose members were known as Quakers.

State Flower

The mountain laurel, *Kalmia latifolia*, was named the state flower in 1933.

State Tree

Tsuga canadensis , the hemlock tree, was adopted as the state tree in 1931. It is also called the eastern hemlock, the Canadian hemlock, the hemlock spruce, the spruce pine, the New England hemlock, and the spruce.

State Beautification and Conservation Plant

The penngift crownvetch, *Voronilla varia*, was designated in 1982.

State Bird

The ruffed grouse, *Bonasa umbellus*, was named state bird in 1931.

State Animal

Adopted in 1959, the state animal is the white-tail deer, *Odocoileus virginianus*.

State Beverage

The state beverage, named in 1982, is milk.

State Dog

The great dane was adopted as the state dog in 1965.

State Fish

The brook trout, *Salvelinus fontinalis*, was designated the state fish in 1970.

State Insect

In 1974 the firefly, *Photinus scintillans*, was adopted as the state insect.

Population

The population of Pennsylvania in 1992 was 12,009,361, and it is the fifth most populous state. There are 267.9 people per square mile—84.8 percent of them in metropolitan areas. About 97 percent of the people of Pennsylvania were born in the United States. Of the foreign-born, the largest groups are the Italians, Poles, Russians, Germans, Austrians, Czechoslovaks, and English. There is also a group that is called "Pennsylvania Dutch" — actually the descendants of

Germans who came to Pennsylvania during the 1600s and 1700s. Some of them still speak a mixture of German and English, and the group includes such religious denominations as the Amish, the Dunkers, and the Mennonites.

Industries

The principal industries of the state are refining steel, and manufacturing apparel and machinery. The chief products are metals, foods, fabricated metal products, and machinery.

Agriculture

The chief crops of the state are corn, hay, mushrooms, apples, potatoes, winter wheat, oats, vegetables, tobacco, and grapes. Pennsylvania is also a livestock state, and there are estimated to be 1.96 million cattle, 800,000 hogs and pigs, 88,000 sheep, and 22.5 million chickens, geese, and turkeys on its farms. Pine, oak, and maple are harvested for timber, and crushed stone, lime, sand, and gravel are important mineral resources. Commercial fishing earned $395,000 in 1992.

Government

The governor is elected to a four-year term, as are the lieutenant governor, the secretary of internal affairs, the state treasurer, and the auditor general. The state legislature, called the general assembly, which meets annually, consists of a 50-member senate and a 203-member house of representatives. Members of both houses are elected from districts divided according to population. The most recent state constitution was adopted in 1873. In addition to its two U.S. senators, Pennsylvania has 21 representatives in the U.S. House of Representatives. The state has 25 votes in the electoral college.

Sports

Many sporting events on the collegiate and secondary school levels are played all

Amish farmers in Lancaster county work the land without the help of modern machinery.

over the state. The first United States women's tennis singles championship was held in Philadelphia in 1887. Several Pennsylvania teams have won the Little League World Series: Maynard of Williamsport (1947), Lock Haven (1948), Morrisville (1954), and Levittown (1960). College football teams have been outstanding. The Orange Bowl was won by Bucknell (1935), Duquesne (1937), and Penn State (1969, 1970, 1974). The Sugar Bowl was won by the University of Pittsburgh (1982) and Penn State (1983). The Cotton Bowl was won twice by Penn State (1972 and 1975).

On the professional level, the Philadelphia Phillies of the National League play baseball at Veterans Stadium, which they share with the Eagles of the National Football League. The Spectrum sports arena is the home of the Philadelphia 76ers of the National Basketball Association and the Flyers of the National Hockey League. The Pittsburgh Pirates of the National League play baseball at Three Rivers Stadium, which they share with the Steelers of the National Football League. The Pittsburgh Penguins of the National Hockey League play their games in the Civic Arena.

Major Cities

Harrisburg (population 52,376). Settled in 1718, the site of the capital of Pennsylvania was first viewed in 1615 by a Frenchman, Étienne Brulé, on a trip down the Susquehanna River. More than a century later John Harris, the first settler, opened a trading post on this spot. In 1785, Harris's son established the town. It became the state capital in 1812, and the cornerstone of the first capitol building was

A cannon at Gettysburg, the site of the decisive civil war battle, immortalized in Lincoln's Gettysburg address.

laid in 1819. The city's main activities include commerce, industry, and state government.

Places to visit in Harrisburg: The Capitol, the North Office Building, the South Office Building, the Forum Building, the Finance Building, the State Museum of Pennsylvania, the Museum of Scientific Discovery, the John Harris Museum (1766), the Dauphin County Courthouse, the Fort Hunter Mansion, and Indian Echo Caverns.

Philadelphia (population 1,585,517). Settled in 1682, William Penn's City of Brotherly Love was really the cradle of the nation. Here the Declaration of Independence was written and adopted, the Constitution was written and signed, the capital of the United States was established, and Washington served most of his years as president.

The first settlers were Quakers who lived in caves dug into the banks of the Delaware River. Within two years, Penn's "greene countrie town" had 600 buildings. The city grew, and was in the forefront of the resistance to the British prior to and during the Revolutionary War. At that time, the most prominent citizen was Benjamin Franklin—the statesman, scientist, diplomat, writer, inventor, and publisher.

Today the city is one of the world's most important ports and contains more than 4,000 factories turning out such products as electrical machinery, appliances, automobile and truck bodies, clothing, carpets, magazines and books, and scientific instruments. It was in Philadelphia that the first American hospital was established. Other American firsts include the first medical college, the first women's medical college, the first bank, the first paper mill, the first steamboat, the first zoo, the first sugar refinery, the first newspaper, the first mint, and the first school for black children.

Places to visit in Philadelphia: Independence Hall, the Jacob Graff House, Liberty Bell Pavilion, Congress Hall, the Old City Hall (1789), Carpenters' Hall (1770), the Bishop White House (1786-1787), the Todd House (1775), the Betsy Ross House, Elfreth's Alley, the Powel House (1765), the Athenaeum of Philadelphia, Cliveden (1767), the United States Mint, the Perelman Antique Toy Museum, the National Museum of American Jewish History, the Norman Rockwell Museum, the Afro-American Historical and Cultural Museum, the Academy of Natural Sciences Museum, the Please Touch Museum for Children, the Rodin Museum, the Philadelphia Museum of Art, the Franklin Institute, the Rosenbach Museum, Penn's Landing, the Gloria Dei Church National Historic Site—"Old Swedes" (1700), St. George's United Methodist Church (1769), Old Pine Street Presbyterian Church

(1768), St. Peter's Church—Episcopal (1761), Old St. Mary's Roman Catholic Church (1763), Christ Church—Episcopal (1695), the Arch Street Friends Meeting House (1804), Fairmount Park, the Zoological Garden, the Schuylkill Valley Nature Center.

Pittsburgh (population 369,879). Settled in 1758, the city was named after William Pitt the elder, the great British statesman. Located where the Allegheny and Monongahela come together to form the Ohio River, it was a strategic port almost from its founding. Today it is the largest inland river port in the United States. Early in the city's history it became a manufacturing city, and its rolling mills turned out nails, axes, frying pans, and shovels for the western settlers. At the end of the Civil War, Pittsburgh was producing half the steel and one-third of the glass made in the country. Today the city, which, because of the amount of industry there, was once called the "Smoky City," has cleaned itself up, and boasts clean air, as well as many gleaming buildings and new high technology industries.

Pittsburgh, once known as the "Smoky City," has undergone tremendous change and redevelopment in recent years.

Places to visit in Pittsburgh: The Monongahela Incline, the Duquesne Incline, the Fort Pitt Museum, the Allegheny County Courthouse, the Station Square Transportation Museum, the Children's Museum, the Carnegie Museum of Natural History, the Carnegie Museum of Art, Phipps Conservatory, the Allegheny Observatory, the Buhl Science Center, the Pittsburgh Zoo, Frick Park, the Historical Society of Western Pennsylvania, the James L. Kelso Bible Lands Museum, the Frick Art Museum, and the Tour-Ed Mine.

Places to Visit

The National Park Service maintains 10 areas in the state of Pennsylvania: Delaware Water Gap National Recreation Area, Fort Necessity National Battlefield, Independence National Historical Park, Gettysburg National Military Park, Eisenhower National Historic Site, Hopewell Furnace National Historic Site, Johnstown Flood National Memorial, Allegheny Portage Railroad National Historic Site, Edgar Allan Poe National Historic Site, and Valley Forge National Historical Park. In addition, there are 72 state recreation areas.

Allentown: George Taylor House and Park. Built in 1768, it was the home of the signer of the Declaration of Independence.

Allenwood: Clyde Peeling's Reptiland. Crocodiles, tortoises, and many varieties of snake can be seen at this specialized zoological attraction.

Altoona: Railroader's Memorial Museum.

Hershey's Chocolate World, a museum of the chocolate industry, stands adjacent to Hersheypark, a popular theme park.

Displays, rolling stock, and artifacts tell of the history of railroading.

Ambridge: Old Economy Village. Here is a six-acre collection of 19th century buildings and houses, built by the Harmony Society, a communal religious colony.

Bear Run: Falling Water. Designed by noted architect Frank Lloyd Wright, this house is built over a waterfall.

Bedford: Espy House. Built in 1770, it was Washington's headquarters during the Whiskey Rebellion of 1794.

Bethlehem: Sun Inn. George Washington, John Adams, and other members of the Continental Congress once stayed at this Moravian inn.

Bird-in-Hand: Amish Village. Here are reconstructed and original buildings of the Amish community.

Bristol: Pennsbury Manor. A reconstruction of William Penn's 17th-century country manor features formal and kitchen gardens.

Cornwall: Cornwall Iron Furnace. This contains an open pit mine (1742-1883) and a miners' village, built

Festivals and reenactments such as this Civil War parade celebrate the state's history.

in 1860.

Doylestown: The Mercer Mile. Dr. Henry Chapman Mercer built three reinforced concrete castles in 1910 which now house the Mercer Museum, a collection of early American tools, Fonthill Museum, Mercer's home, and the Moravian Pottery and Tile Works.

Easton: First United Church of Christ. Build in 1776, it served as a hospital during the Revolutionary War.

Elkins Park: Beth Sholom. This is the only synagogue designed by Frank Lloyd Wright.

Ephrata: Ephrata Cloisters. The unadorned buildings in the German medieval style once housed an unusual religious community.

Erie: Flagship Niagara. This brig, which served as Commodore Oliver Hazard Perry's flagship in the Battle of Lake Erie (1813), was restored in 1988.

Franklin: Antique Music Museum. Here is a collection of nickelodeons, band organs, and many other antique instruments.

Gettysburg: Gettysburg National Military Park. The battlefield includes the sites of Pickett's Charge, Little Round Top, and Devil's Den, as well as the cemetery and many stone monuments.

Hamburg: Hawk Mountain Bird Sanctuary. Eagle and hawk flights are visible from this bird sanctuary.

Hershey: Hershey's Chocolate World. Here can be seen the steps of chocolate production from bean to candy.

Huntingdon: Lincoln Caverns. A 50-minute tour includes two caves.

Kennett Square: Longwood Gardens. These magnificent gardens are on the former estate of Pierre S. du Pont.

King of Prussia: Harriton House. Built in 1704, it was the home of Charles Thompson, secretary of the Continental Congresses.

Kulpsville: Morgan Log House. Built in 1695, it was the home of the grandfather of Daniel Boone and General Robert Morgan, and is the oldest surviving medieval-style log house in the country.

Lancaster: Wheatland. Built in 1828, this was the home of President James Buchanan.

Mount Pocono: Memorytown, USA. This old-time village includes many business establishments of long ago.

New Hope: Parry Mansion. Built in 1784, it is a restored stone house with 11 rooms on view.

Orbisonia: East Broad Top Railroad. This is the last narrow-gauge railroad operating east of the Mississippi.

Pottstown: Pottsgrove Mansion. Built in 1752, it was the home of John Potts, an ironmaster and founder of the town.

Reading: The Pagoda. This observation tower was originally designed as a hotel and anchored to a mountain by ten tons of bolts.

Scranton: Steamtown, USA. Here is one of the nation's largest collections of steam locomotives.

Shartlesville: Roadside America. This miniature village contains scenes re-creating 200 years of rural American life.

Stroudsburg: Quiet Valley Living Historical Farm. Demonstrations of seasonal farm activities take place among 13 original or reconstructed buildings of the 18th century.

Uniontown: Laurel Caverns. This cave tour includes a tram ride.

Valley Forge: National Historic Park. This was the site of The Continental Army's camp during the winter of 1777-1778.

Washington Crossing: McConkey Ferry Inn. Built in 1752, the historic inn has been restored.

Wrightsville: Donegal Mills Plantation and Inn. Dating from 1800, this village was first laid out in 1736.

York: Friends Meeting House. Quaker meetings have been held here since 1766.

Events

There are many events and organizations that schedule activities of various kinds in the state of Pennsylvania. Here are some of them.

Sports: Sled Dog Races (Bloomsburg), Susquehanna River Fishing Tournament (Bloomsburg), Bowhunter's Festival (Galeton), Kipona (Harrisburg), Eastern Sports and Outdoor Show (Harrisburg), Pennsylvania National Horse Show (Harrisburg), Standardbred Horse Sale (Harrisburg), Sports and Energy Show (Huntingdon), automobile racing at Pocono International Raceway (Mount Pocono), University of Pennsylvania Relay (Philadelphia), Devon Horse Show (Philadelphia), Army-Navy Football Game (Philadelphia), Horse racing at Philadelphia Park (Philadelphia), canoe races (Port Allegaey), Saint Ubaldo Day (Scranton), National Pike Festival (Washington), harness racing at The Meadows (Washington), Harness racing at Pocono Downs (Wilkes-Barre), Tiadaghton Elm Classic Canoe Racing (Williamsport) Slowpitch Softball Tournament (Williamsport), All Breed Dog Show and National Obedience Trials (Williamsport), Little League World Series (Williamsport), boat regatta (Williamsport).

Arts and Crafts: Das Awkscht Fescht (Allentown), Super Sunday (Allentown), Blair County Arts Festival (Altoona), Old Bedford Village Craft Festival (Bedford), Moravian Antiques Show (Bethlehem), Covered Bridge and Arts Festival (Bloomsburg), Western Pennsylvania Laurel Festival (Brookville), Dankfest (Harmony), Laurel Blossom Festival (Jim Thorpe), Fort Armstrong Folk Festival (Kittanning), Folk Festival (Kutztown), Craft Days (Lancaster), Harvest Days (Lancaster), Fort Ligonier Days (Ligonier), Beech Creek Bean Soup Festival (Lock Haven), Phillips Mill Community

The Pennsylvania Philharmonic Orchestra.

Association Art Exhibition (New Hope), Flower Show (Philadelphia), Head House Open Air Craft Market (Philadelphia), Phipps Conservatory Flower Shows (Pittsburgh), Three Rivers Arts Festival (Pittsburgh), Duryea Day Antique and Classic Auto Meet (Pottstown), Mountain Craft Days (Somerset), Springs Folk Festival (Springs), Central Pennsylvania Festival of the Arts (State College), Pocono Mountains Antique Show (Stroudsburg), Covered Bridge Weekend Festival (Washington),

Antique Auto Show (Williamsport), River Walk Art Festival (York).

Music: Drum Corps International-Eastern Regional Championship (Allentown), Bedford Springs Festival for the Performing Arts (Bedford), Bach Festival (Bethlehem), Musikfest (Bethlehem), Old Fiddlers' Picnic (Downingtown), Erie Philharmonic (Erie), Franklin Silver Cornet Band Concerts (Franklin), Harrisburg Symphony (Harrisburg), Banjo Pickin' Contest at Raystown Lake (Huntingdon), Music at

Gretna (Lancaster), Mummers Parade (Philadelphia), American Music Theater Festival (Philadelphia), Philadelphia Orchestra (Philadelphia), Concerto Soloists Chamber

Entertainment: Bavarian Summer Festival (Adamstown), Summer Celebration (Allentown), Balloon Festival (Allentown), Great Allentown Fair (Allentown), Keystone Country Festival (Altoona), Nationality Days (Ambridge), Great Bedford County Fair (Bedford), Fall Foliage Festival (Bedford), Shad Festival (Bethlehem), Christmas (Bethlehem), Live Bethlehem Orchestra (Philadelphia), Pennsylvania Opera Theater (Philadelphia), Opera Company of Philadelphia (Philadelphia), Mann Music Center (Philadelphia), Robin Hood Dell East (Philadelphia), Pennsylvania Ballet (Philadelphia), Philly Pops (Philadelphia), Pittsburgh Symphony (Pittsburgh), Pittsburgh Opera (Pittsburgh), Pittsburgh Civic Light Opera (Pittsburgh), Reading Symphony (Reading).

Christmas Pageant (Bethlehem), Bloomsburg Fair (Bloomsburg), Crook Farm County Fair (Bradford), Fallsington Day (Bristol), Cumberland County Fair (Carlisle), Franklin County

Fair (Chambersburg), Clarion River Country Days (Clarion), Autumn Leaf Festival (Clarion), Clearfield County Fair (Clearfield), Historic Schaefferstown Events (Cornwall), Street Fair (Ephrata), Rocky Grove Fair (Franklin), Bark Peeler's Convention (Galeton), Woodsmen's Carnival (Galeton), Germania Old Home Day (Galeton), Apple Blossom Weekend (Gettysburg), Civil War Heritage Days (Gettysburg), South Mountain Fair (Gettysburg), Apple Harvest Festival (Gettysburg), Pennsylvania State Farm Show (Harrisburg), All American Dairy Show and Pennsylvania Junior Dairy Show (Harrisburg), Pennsylvania Livestock Exposition (Harrisburg), Chocolate Festival (Hershey), Antique Automobile Club (Hershey), Christmas in Hershey (Hershey), Wayne County Fair (Honesdale), Hartslog Day (Huntingdon), Mary Packer Cummings Weekend (Jim Thorpe), Victorian Wedding Celebration (Jim Thorpe), Carbon County Fair (Jim Thorpe), Heritage Day (Jim Thorpe), Fall Foliage Festival (Jim Thorpe), Bologna Fest (Lebanon), Mifflin County Goose Day Celebration (Lewiston), Ligonier Highland Games and Gathering of the

Clans of Scotland (Ligonier), Flaming Foliage Festival (Lock Haven), Rose Festival (Manheim), Pennsylvania Renaissance Faire (Manheim), Crawford County Fair (Meadville), County Fair (Meyersdale), Cherry Festival (North East), Wine County Harvest Festival (North East), Elfreth's Alley Fete Day (Philadelphia), Freedom Festival (Philadelphia), Thanksgiving Day Parade (Philadelphia), Folk Festival (Pittsburgh), Heritage Celebration (Reading), La Fiesta Italiana (Scranton), Maple Festival (Somerset), Somerfest (Somerset), Farmers' and Threshermen's Jubilee (Somerset), Centre County Grange Fair (State College), National Pike Festival (Uniontown), Fayette County Fair (Uniontown), Fayette County Fall Foliage Celebration (Uniontown), Washington County Fair (Washington), "The Crossing" (Washington Crossing Historical Park), Pennsylvania State Laurel Festival (Wellsboro), Cherry Blossom Festival (Wilkes-Barre), Dallas Fall Fair (Wilkes-Barre), Luzerne County Folk Festival (Wilkes-Barre), Susquehanna Boom Festival (Williamsport), Lycoming County Fair (Williamsport), Olde York Street Fair (York), York Interstate Fair

(York).

Tours: Laurel Tour (Clearfield), Holley Ross Pottery (Cresco), Hibernia Mansion Candlelight Tour (Downingtown), Historic House Tour (Harmony), Christmas Open House (Harmony), Historic Lancaster Walking Tour (Lancaster), L. E. Smith Glass Company (New Stanton), Philadelphia Open House (Philadelphia), Fairmont Park Historical Christmas Tours (Philadelphia).

Theater: Bloomsburg Theatre Ensemble (Bloomsburg), Boal Barn Playhouse (Boalsburg), Totem Pole Playhouse (Chambersburg), Pocono Playhouse (Cresco), "Vorspeil" (Ephrata), Fulton Opera House (Lancaster), Mountain Playhouse (Ligonier), Saint Vincent Summer Theatre (Ligonier), Millbrook Playhouse (Lock Haven), Pocono Playhouse (Mountainhome), Bucks County Playhouse (New Hope), Philadelphia Company (Philadelphia), Philadelphia Drama Guild (Philadelphia), Walnut Street Theatre (Philadelphia), Pittsburgh Public Theater (Pittsburgh), Pennsylvania Centre State (University Park), Pennsylvania State University Resident Theatre Company (University Park).

The sun sets over Lake Erie, which borders Pennsylvania on its northwestern tip.

The Land and the Climate

Pennsylvania lies in the center of the Appalachian Mountains. It is bordered by Delaware, Maryland, and West Virginia on the south, West Virginia and Ohio on the west, Lake Erie and New York on the north, and New Jersey on the east. The state has seven main land regions. They are, from west to east: the Erie Lowland, the Appalachian Plateau, the Appalachian Ridge and Valley Region, the Blue Ridge, the Piedmont, the New England Upland, and the Atlantic Coastal Plain.

The Erie Lowland, a narrow strip in northwestern Pennsylvania along the shores of Lake Erie, was once part of the lake bed. This flat, sandy region supports vegetable and fruit crops, especially grapes.

The Appalachian Plateau is part of a land elevation that extends from New York to Alabama. In Pennsylvania it is also called the Allegheny Plateau, for the Allegheny Mountains that make up the western part of the Appalachian chain. The plateau includes the entire northern and western portions of the state, except for the Erie Lowland strip. It is a region of deep, narrow valleys and flat-topped divides (land regions from which rivers flow in opposite directions). In the north are glacial rocks and boulders, and in the north-central section are plateaus that rise more than 2,000 feet above sea level. These plateaus slope gradually to the east, west, and southwest. The highest point in Pennsylvania, 3,213-foot Mount Davis, is located in Somerset County. In the western part of the Appalachian Plateau are coal, gas, and oil fields. The area is also a region of dairy and cattle farms, with some truck (vegetable) farming and maple-syrup manufacturing.

The Delaware Water Gap is a deep, 2.5-mile-long gorge cut through the Appalachian Mountains by the Delaware River. The dramatic scenery of this area is one of the state's most spectacular tourist attractions.

White-water rafting is a popular sport in the Pocono Mountains. The Pocono area, on the eastern border of Pennsylvania, is one of the busiest resorts on the East Coast.

The Appalachian Ridge and Valley Region is part of a highland that extends from New York to Alabama; in Pennsylvania, it forms a curved strip south of the Appalachian Plateau. The border between these two regions is called the Allegheny Front. Wheat and oat crops and poultry and dairy farms flourish here. Along the southern and eastern boundaries of this region is an area called the Great Valley, which combines the Cumberland, Lebanon, and Lehigh Valleys with their fertile farmland. The hard-coal, or anthracite, and slate regions of Pennsylvania are in the eastern part of the Appalachian Ridge and Valley Region.

The Blue Ridge is named for the Blue Ridge Mountains, which run from southern Pennsylvania to Georgia. In Pennsylvania, the Blue Ridge is a narrow, finger-shaped region at the state's south-central border. It is primarily a land of forests and includes part of Gettysburg National Military Park.

The hilly Piedmont extends from New Jersey to Alabama; in Pennsylvania, it covers most of the southeastern part of the state. The Piedmont's rich plains, valleys, and low hills are filled with prosperous cattle, dairy, poultry, and truck farms.

The New England Upland extends from Pennsylvania, where it is a narrow rectangle in the eastern part of the state, to Maine. The Upland ridge crosses scenic Berks, Bucks, Lehigh, and Northampton Counties.

The Atlantic Coastal Plain is part of the shelflike lowland that reaches from New York to southern Florida. In the southeastern corner of Pennsylvania, it is a narrow strip of land whose flat, fertile fields produce a variety of vegetables. The historic port city of Philadelphia is in this region.

The principal rivers of eastern and central Pennsylvania are the Delaware, Lehigh, Schuylkill, Susquehanna, Juniata, Allegheny, and Monongahela. Western Pennsylvania is drained by the great Ohio River system. Some of the most spectacular waterfalls in the East tumble over cliffs in the Pocono Mountains, a popular vacation area.

Lake Conneaut is the largest natural lake that is entirely within Pennsylvania's borders. Larger still is man-made Lake Wallenpaupack, which covers nine square miles in the northeast.

Pennsylvania temperatures are affected by the state's moist climate, which produces cold winters and warm summers. There is considerable variance between the eastern and western parts of the state, especially in the amount of snowfall, which is much higher in the northwest. Average January temperatures are between 26 and 32 degrees Fahrenheit; in July, they range from 70 to 76 degrees F. Rainfall is plentiful and conducive to agriculture: 34 to 51 inches in western Pennsylvania, and 40 to 46 inches in the eastern half of the state.

Almost all of Pennsylvania lies within the Appalachian Highlands region of the United States. The many plateaus, highlands, and mountains that curve in a chain from the northeast to the south-central part of the state give its scenery a wonderful variety and beauty.

Pennsylvania possesses a charming mix of the old and the new. Bustling cities such as Philadelphia offer all the advantages of a modern metropolis yet retain a colorful slice of their colonial history. Countrified areas like Lancaster, where Amish farmers strictly maintain their traditional lifestyle, provide a glimpse of a simpler time.

William Penn, an English Quaker, received his title to Pennsylvania in 1681 in payment of a debt that was owed to his father by King Charles II. The king called the grant Pennsylvania, or "Penn's Wood," in honor of the elder Penn, an English admiral. Penn established Philadelphia, the "city of brotherly love," in 1682 as an experiment in religious tolerance. The settlement attracted so many people that it quickly became the largest city in colonial America.

The History

Before settlers from Europe arrived in what is now Pennsylvania, Indians of the Eastern forests had been living there for hundreds of years, hunting, farming, and fishing. When the white men came, they found Algonkian and Iroquoian Indians dwelling in semi-permanent communities that relocated when fish or game grew sparse. The Algonkian tribes included the Conoy, the Delaware, the Nanticoke, and the Shawnee, who lived in round or oval wigwams built of saplings and elm bark. The Pennsylvania Iroquois tribe was the Susquehannock, who lived along the Susquehanna River in wooden "long houses" surrounded by stockades.

In 1609 Henry Hudson, the English explorer, arrived in Delaware Bay. He had been employed by the Dutch East India Company to seek a route to the Far East. Hudson and his men were probably the first Europeans to see a part of Pennsylvania, and his reports about the region generated interest among the Dutch, who sent other explorers. In 1615 the Dutch captain Cornelius Hendricksen sailed up the Delaware to the present site of Philadelphia. Although these voyages had established a Dutch claim to the land that lined the Delaware River, the Dutch did little to colonize the country beyond establishing trading posts here and there. It was Johan Printz, with his Swedish settlers, who first put down roots at a village called New Gottenburg, on Tinicum Island, in 1643. This settlement, near what is now Philadelphia, became the capital of New Sweden. In 1655 Dutch troops from New Netherland (now New York), under the command of Peter Stuyvesant, captured New Sweden. The Dutch held the region until 1664, when it was taken over by the British.

The English Duke of York controlled the Pennsylvania region until 1681. In that year, all the land between the 41st and 43rd latitudes and extending west five degrees from the Delaware River line was granted to William Penn by Charles II of England. He presented the Quaker leader with a charter that made him proprietor of "Pennsylvania," or "Penn's Woods" (although Penn had originally wanted to name the territory New Wales). Penn had received the grant in payment of a royal debt to his father, an English admiral.

Penn landed in 1682 and invested the land with his money, liberal ideas of leadership, and fellow Quakers who had suffered religious persecution in England. He had a supplemental charter for the Lower Counties—the land that would become Delaware and part of Maryland. The landing was made at Upland (now Chester), and Penn set up a capital, laid plans for a city at Philadelphia, befriended and traded with the Indians, and established an elected legislature. He had already drafted a "Frame of Government" whose most important provision was the one that guaranteed religious freedom.

A perspective of Philadelphia from the east in 1731. Throughout the 18th century, the city rivaled Boston as the political and cultural center of the colonies. It became, after London, the largest city in the British Empire.

The Declaration of Independence was adopted in Philadelphia on July 4, 1776, by the Continental Congress of the 13 North American colonies. It set forth their reasons for claiming independence from Great Britain and formalized the creation of the United States. The Declaration was outlined by Thomas Jefferson, John Adams, and Benjamin Franklin, and written by Jefferson. The famous painting below, by John Trumbull, shows Jefferson presenting the Declaration to the Congress. Benjamin Franklin is on his left.

The Swedes, Finns, and Dutch who were already in the Pennsylvania territory were granted citizenship. They were soon joined by Welsh, German, Scotch, Irish, and French Huguenot immigrants. Of these, the Germans left the strongest imprint on the state.

Shortly after he arrived in the colony, Penn made a formal treaty of friendship with the Indians and paid them for the land that King Charles had deeded to him.

Trouble started in 1684 when Penn returned to England, leaving his deputy governor in charge. Members of the general assembly began to resent laws originated by the provincial council (the upper house of the legislature) and delayed action on passing them. Then King James II of England, a close friend of Penn's, was overthrown in 1688. James's daughter Mary and her husband, Prince William of Orange, became the rulers of Great Britain, and they distrusted Penn because of his close ties to the former king. Penn's right to govern his colony was handed over to the governor of New York in 1692. The following year, however, Penn was able to convince William and Mary of his loyalty, and he was restored to his governorship in 1694.

In Philadelphia, George Washington presided over the Constitutional Convention of 1787. It convened to amend the Articles of Confederation, but produced instead an almost entirely new framework for American government. Fifty-five of the nation's most prominent statesmen, after much debate about representation for the states, drafted what we know as the Constitution of the United States. Upon this document we base our entire system of government and law.

Penn returned to the New World in 1699 and wrote a new constitution, called the "Charter of Privileges." This made the general assembly the chief law-making body in the colony and gave greater control of the government to the people.

Penn went back to England in 1701 and died there in 1718. But his family continued to govern the colony until the Revolutionary War. The pre-Revolution years were characterized by growing distrust and resentment on the part of the Indians and dissatisfaction with British colonial policy. When war did come, Philadelphia was at the heart of it. The First Continental Congress met there to protest the Stamp Act in 1774. The Second Continental Congress met in 1775, after the war broke out, to draw up the Declaration of Independence and take steps toward forming the first federal government of the United States. When the British threatened Philadelphia in 1776, after the Declaration of Independence was adopted, the legislature took up temporary residence in Baltimore, Lancaster, and finally York, where it drafted the Articles of Confederation. In 1787 the Constitutional Convention met in Philadelphia, and Pennsylvania became the second state to ratify the United States Constitution. Philadelphia became the nation's capital until the government moved south to Washington, D.C., the new city on the Potomac, in 1800.

Revolutionary War cannons at Valley Forge. It was here that General George Washington's army spent the bitterly cold winter of 1777–78 while the British occupied Philadelphia. Washington's army was poorly fed and clothed, unprepared for the severe weather that caused many deaths at Valley Forge.

The Brandywine River Museum is near the Revolutionary War site where American troops suffered a crushing defeat in 1777.

In spite of its peace-loving Quaker heritage, Pennsylvania has found itself in the thick of every war ever fought in what is now the United States. Both Fort Necessity and Fort Duquesne were important in the French and Indian Wars. During the Revolution, British troops marched into Pennsylvania in September 1777 and defeated General George Washington in the Battle of Brandywine. The British then killed many American soldiers in the Paoli Massacre outside Philadelphia, capturing the city shortly afterward.

Washington's bitterest winter encampment was at Valley Forge, where his ill-clad troops suffered from cold and hunger. And it was from Pennsylvania that he launched his Christmas night attack on Hessian mercenaries across the Delaware River in Trenton, New Jersey. Settlers in the Wyoming Valley, in present-day Luzerne County, were massacred in a fort near what is now Wilkes-Barre in 1778 by a combined force of British soldiers and Indians.

The Revolution was barely over when Pennsylvania farmers who made whiskey from their grain staged the Whiskey Rebellion in 1794, testing the power of the new federal government to enforce its laws within the states. The federal tax on whiskey was maintained despite the opposition of the Pennsylvanians. The state continued to prosper in agriculture, commerce, and industry. During the War of 1812 with Great Britain, a Pennsylvania admiral named Oliver Hazard Perry launched ships built in his state from a Pennsylvania port (Erie) to fight the Battle of the Great Lakes.

In the mid-1850s Pennsylvania became one of the hubs of the nation's industrial growth. The Ohio and Mississippi Canal and the Schuylkill Canal had been opened. Development of the hard-coal deposits in the state had led to improvements in Pennsylvania's hundred-year-old iron-making industry. Railroads had been built all over the state, and the steamboats developed by John Fitch and Robert Fulton were carrying goods on the country's waterways. In 1859 the first oil well was drilled near Titusville. By 1860 Pittsburgh had become an important industrial center and was called "the Gateway to the West," while Philadelphia was one of the nation's leading manufacturing cities.

Far left:
Independence Hall, formerly the Pennsylvania State House, witnessed the signing of both the Declaration of Independence and the Constitution of the United States.

At left:
The Liberty Bell is housed at Philadelphia's Independence Hall. It first rang to proclaim the signing of the Declaration of Independence and announced other important events in the years that followed. The bell was made in England in 1752 and cracked soon after its arrival. Recasting solved the problem for some years, but the bell finally broke while tolling for the funeral rites of Chief Justice John Marshall in 1835. Today it serves as a silent symbol of America's freedom.

The Battle of Gettysburg was fought from July 1 to 3, 1863, after General Robert E. Lee led a Confederate army of some 75,000 men into Pennsylvania. Three days of fierce fighting ended in Lee's retreat to Virginia with Union General George G. Meade in cautious pursuit. In total, the Union lost 23,000 men—killed, wounded, or missing in action—and the Confederacy almost 28,000.

Because of their Quaker heritage, most Pennsylvanians opposed slavery, and the state gave strong support to the Union during the Civil War (1861–65). Some 340,000 men from the Keystone State went to war—only New York sent more troops. Civil War battles crossed into Pennsylvania three times, and one of them—the Battle of Gettysburg—turned the tide of the war in the Union's favor. On November 19, 1863, President Abraham Lincoln dedicated part of the Gettysburg battlefield as a cemetery for those who had died there, delivering his famous Gettysburg Address.

Pennsylvania continued to prosper after the war, and many new industries, including oil and aluminum, were established in the state. Pittsburgh became a national leader in steel production. By the turn of the century more than half the people in Pennsylvania were living in cities and towns, to which they had been drawn by the booming industries. At the time, Pennsylvania supplied most of the nation's coal and manufactured about 60 percent of its steel.

World War I solidified Pennsylvania's reputation as a mining and manufacturing state; it contributed high levels of both military goods and manpower to the war effort between 1917 and 1918. But the Great Depression of the 1930s hit Pennsylvania harder than most states, because of its dependence on manufacturing. Hundreds of thousands were out of work, but state and federal projects in road-building, reforestation, and conservation helped alleviate economic distress.

During World War II the state's factories and shipyards returned to military production, and economic growth continued after the war. Huge new steel mills were built, and the first full-scale nuclear-power reactor for civilian purposes was opened at Shippingport in 1957. Pennsylvania today is still one of the country's most important manufacturing and mining states, despite the decline of the anthracite coal industry. The state has diversified into large-scale manufacture of apparel, food products, and machinery, in addition to basic metals like iron and steel. Tourism has become a successful business in Pennsylvania—in 1985, out-of-state tourists spent $8.9 billion.

Education

Education has always been important in Pennsylvania: it began when the first settlers moved in. In the 1640s, Swedish Lutheran ministers were teaching children in Tinicum, the state's first settlement. Pennsylvania's first colonial constitution stated, in 1682, that children should know how to read and write by the time they were 12 years old. The Friends' public school in Philadelphia, founded by the Quakers in 1689, still exists as the William Penn Charter School.

By the end of the 1700s, there were six institutions of higher education in Pennsylvania: the University of Pennsylvania (1740), Moravian College (1742), Dickinson College (1773), Washington and Jefferson College (1782), the University of Pittsburgh (1787), and Franklin and Marshall College (1787). Today Pennsylvania has more than 80 colleges and universities. Benjamin Franklin founded

The Pittsburgh area has long been one of the largest industrial centers on the eastern seaboard. Best known for its production of steel, it has also been a key center for coal mining and other mineral industries.

Far left:
Benjamin Franklin is probably Philadelphia's most famous citizen. After he arrived from Boston, his birthplace, in 1723, he became such a successful printer and publisher that he was able to pursue his interests in science and politics. He invented bifocal glasses and the Franklin stove and carried out his famous experiment with a kite in a thunderstorm to prove that lightning was electricity. Franklin's diplomacy and statesmanship were invaluable to the young United States.

Above left:
American soldier and Indian fighter Anthony Wayne was born in Chester County. His victory over confederated Indian tribes at the Battle of Fallen Timbers in 1794 opened much of the Northwest Territory to settlement.

the Library Company of Philadelphia—the first subscription library in the colonies—in 1731. The oldest art school in the United States, the Pennsylvania Academy of the Fine Arts in Philadelphia, was founded in 1805. And the Academy of Natural Sciences in Philadelphia, established in 1812, is the nation's oldest institution of natural sciences. In 1834 the legislature approved an act providing free public schools throughout the state.

The People

Today, approximately 93 percent of Pennsylvanians live in metropolitan areas, of which Philadelphia and Pittsburgh are the largest cities. Other important cities include Allentown, Bethlehem, Erie, Scranton, Reading, and Lancaster. About 94 percent of Pennsylvania's residents were born in the United States.

Famous People

Many famous people were born in the State of Pennsylvania. Here are a few:

Louisa May Alcott 1832-1888, Germantown. Novelist: *Little Women*

Christian B. Alfinsen b.1916, Monessen. Nobel Prize-winning biochemist

Marian Anderson b.1902, Philadelphia. Operatic contralto

Maxwell Anderson 1888-1959, Atlantic. Pulitzer Prize-winning playwright: *High Tor, The Bad Seed*

Henry "Hap" Arnold 1886-1950, Gladwyne. World War II Air Force general

Frankie Avalon b.1940, Philadelphia. Pop singer

Carroll Baker b.1931, Johnstown. Movie actress: *Harlow*

Samuel Barber 1910-1981, West Chester. Classical composer

Ethel Barrymore 1879-1959, Philadelphia. Academy Award-winning actress: *None But the Lonely Heart*

John Barrymore 1882-1942, Philadelphia. Shakespearean actor

Lionel Barrymore 1878-1954, Philadelphia. Movie actor: *It's a Wonderful Life*

Donald Barthelme 1931-1989, Philadelphia. Novelist: *Great Acts*

Stephen Vincent Benet 1898-1943, Bethlehem. Pulitzer Prize-winning poet: *John Brown's Body*

James G. Blaine 1830-1893, West Brownsville. Senator and secretary of state

George Blanda b.1927, Youngwood. Hall of Fame football player

David Brenner b.1945, Philadelphia. Stand-up comic

Charles Bronson b.1922, Ehrenfield. Movie actor: *Death Wish*

James Buchanan 1791-1868, Cove Gap. Fifteenth president of the United States

Alexander Calder 1898-1976, Philadelphia. Sculptor and printmaker

Roy Campanella 1921-93, Philadelphia. Hall of Fame baseball player

John Dickson Carr 1906-1976, Uniontown. Mystery writer: *The Bride of Newgate*

Rachel Carson 1907-1964, Springdale. Writer on the environment and ecology: *Silent Spring*

Mary Cassatt 1844-1926, Allegheny City. Painter and printmaker

George Catlin 1796-1872, Wilkes-Barre. Painter

Wilt Chamberlain b.1936, Philadelphia. Hall of Fame basketball player

Chubby Checker b.1941, Philadelphia. Pop singer

Noam Chomsky b.1928, Philadelphia. Linguist

Henry Steele Commager b.1902, Pittsburgh. Historian

Perry Como b.1912, Canonsburg. Pop singer

Charles Conrad, Jr. b.1930, Philadelphia. Astronaut

Bill Cosby b.1937,

Philadelphia. Stand-up comic and actor

Jim Croce 1941-1973, Philadelphia. Folk-rock singer

Blythe Danner b.1945, Philadelphia. Movie actress: *Brighton Beach Memoirs*

Tony Dorsett b.1954, Aliquippa. Football player

Jimmy Dorsey 1904-1957, Shenandoah. Band leader

Tommy Dorsey 1905-1956, Shenandoah. Band leader

Paul Douglas 1907-1959,

Philadelphia. Movie actor: *A Letter to Three Wives*

Thomas Eakins 1844-1916, Philadelphia. Painter

Fabian b.1943, Philadelphia. Pop singer

W. C. Fields 1880-1946, Philadelphia. Stage and screen comic

Eddie Fisher b.1928, Philadelphia. Pop singer

Stephen Foster 1826-1864, Lawrenceville. Song writer

Nellie Fox 1927-1975, Saint Thomas. Hall of Fame

baseball player

Robert Fulton 1765-1815, Little Britain. Inventor of the practical steamboat

Thomas H. Gallaudet 1787-1851, Philadelphia. Founder of the first free school for the deaf in the United States

Erroll Garner 1921-1977, Pittsburgh. Jazz pianist

Stan Getz 1927-91, Philadelphia. Jazz tenor saxophonist

Martha Graham 1894-1991, Pittsburgh. Dancer and choreographer

Red Grange 1903-91, Folksville. Hall of Fame football player

Charles Grodin b.1935, Pittsburgh. Movie actor: *Rosemary's Baby*

Winfield Scott Hancock 1824-1886, Montgomery County. Civil War Union general

Henry J. Heinz 1844-1919, Pittsburgh. Founder of H. J. Heinz food company

Philip S. Hench 1896-1965, Pittsburgh. Nobel Prize-winning physiologist

Milton S. Hershey 1857-1945,

Martha Graham was one of the earliest and most creative choreographers in the modern dance movement.

Grace Kelly's marriage to Prince Rainier of Monaco marked the end of her movie career.

Dauphin County. Founder of Hershey Chocolate Company

Edwards Hicks 1780-1849, Attleboro. Folk painter

Hedda Hopper 1890-1966, Hollidaysburg. Movie columnist

Marilyn Horne b. 1934, Bradford. Mezzo-soprano

Reggie Jackson b.1946, Wyncote. Baseball player

Robert H. Jackson 1892-1954, Spring Creek. Supreme Court justice

Robinson Jeffers 1887-1962, Pittsburgh. Pulitzer Prize-winning poet: *Hungerford and Other Poems*

Shirley Jones b.1934, Smithtown. Academy Award-winning actress: *Elmer Gantry*

George S. Kaufman 1889-1961, Pittsburgh. Pulitzer Prize-winning playwright: *You Can't Take It With You*

Gene Kelly b.1912, Pittsburgh. Movie actor and director: *Singin' in the Rain*

Grace Kelly 1929-1981, Philadelphia. Academy Award-winning actress: *The Country Girl*

Jean Kerr b.1923, Scranton. Novelist and playwright: *Please Don't Eat the Daisies*

Jack Klugman b.1922, Philadelphia. Three-time Emmy Award-winning actor: *The Odd Couple*

Maxine Kumin b.1925, Philadelphia. Pulitzer Prize-winning poet: *Up Country*

Patti LaBelle b.1944, Philadelphia. Rock singer

Mario Lanza 1921-1959, Philadelphia. Tenor and movie actor

Richard Lester b.1932, Philadelphia. Director: *The Three Musketeers*

Sidney Lumet b.1924, Philadelphia. Director: *Network*

Sparky Lyle b.1944, DuBois. Baseball pitcher

Charles MacArthur 1895-1956, Scranton. Playwright and journalist: *The Front Page*

Jeanette MacDonald 1907-1965, Philadelphia. Soprano and movie actress

John D. MacDonald 1916–1986, Sharon. Novelist: *Condominium*

Joseph L. Mankiewicz b.1909, Wilkes-Barre. Director: *Cleopatra*

Pete Maravich 1948-1988, Aliquippa. Basketball player

George C. Marshall 1880-1959, Uniontown. World War II general and secretary of state

Al Martino b.1927, Philadelphia. Pop singer

Christy Mathewson 1880-

Arnold Palmer received his first golf club at the age of three.

1925, Factoryville. Hall of Fame baseball pitcher

George McClellan 1826-1885, Philadelphia. Civil War Union general

William M. McGuffey 1800-1873, Claysville. Author of the McGuffey's Readers

Jim McKay b.1921, Philadelphia. Television sportscaster

Charles McKim 1847-1909, Chester County. Architect

Margaret Mead 1901-1978, Philadelphia. Anthropologist

Anna Moffo b. 1927, Wayne. Soprano

Earl Monroe b.1944, Philadelphia. Basketball player

John P. Muhlenberg 1746-1807, Trappe. Revolutionary War general

Stan Musial b.1920, Donora. Hall of Fame baseball player

Joe Namath b.1943, Beaver Falls. Hall of Fame football player

Clifford Odets 1906-1963, Philadelphia. Playwright: *The Country Girl*

John O'Hara 1905-1970, Pottsville. Novelist: *Butterfield 8*

Jack Palance b.1920, Lattimer Mills. Movie actor: *Shane*

Arnold Palmer b.1929, Youngstown. Champion golfer

Maxfield Parrish 1870-1966, Philadelphia. Painter

Robert E. Peary 1856-1920, Cresson. Arctic explorer

Arthur Penn b.1922, Philadelphia. Director: *Little Big Man*

David Dixon Porter 1813-1891, Chester. Civil War Union admiral

Man Ray 1890-1976, Philadelphia. Painter, sculptor, photographer

Mary Roberts Rinehart 1876-1958, Pittsburgh. Mystery writer: *The Spiral Staircase*

Todd Rungren b.1950, Philadelphia. Rock singer

Bayard Rustin 1910-1987,

In 1909, Robert Peary led the first successful expedition to the North Pole.

Gertrude Stein spent most of her adult life in Paris, returning to the United States only once, in 1934.

West Chester. Civil rights activist

Bobby Rydell b.1942, Philadelphia. Pop singer

David O. Selznick 1902-1965, Pittsburgh. Producer: *Gone With the Wind*

John French Sloan 1871-1951, Lock Haven. Painter

William D. Snodgrass b.1926, Wilkinsburg. Pulitzer Prize-winning

poet: *Heart's Needle*

Carl Spaatz 1891-1974, Boyertown. World War II Air Force general

Gertrude Stein 1874-1946, Allegheny. Novelist: *Three Lives*

Wallace Stevens 1879-1955, Reading. Pulitzer Prize-winning poet: *Collected Poems*

James Stewart b.1908, Indiana. Academy Award-winning actor: *The Philadelphia Story*

Clement Studebaker 1831-1901, Gettysburg. Co-founder of Studebaker auto firm

Jacqueline Susann 1921-1974, Philadelphia. Novelist: *The Valley of the Dolls*

Ida Tarbell 1857-1944, Erie County. Muckraking journalist

Paul Taylor b.1930, Allegheny County. Dancer and choreographer

Howard M. Temin b.1934, Philadelphia. Nobel Prize-winning molecular

biologist

Bill Tilden 1893-1953, Germantown. Champion tennis player

Johnny Unitas b.1933, Pittsburgh. Hall of Fame football player

John Updike b.1932, Shillington. Novelist: *Rabbit, Run*

Bobby Vinton b.1935, Canonsburg. Pop singer

Honus Wagner 1874-1955, Mansfield. Hall of Fame baseball player

Joseph Wambaugh b. 1937, East Pittsburgh. Novelist:

Ethel Waters was the first female singer to receive permission to perform W.C. Handy's classic "St. Louis Blues."

The Blue Knight
Joseph Wanamaker 1838-1922, Philadelphia. Founder of Wanamaker's department store
Andy Warhol 1928-1987, Pittsburgh. Pop artist
Ethel Waters 1900-1977, Chester. Blues singer
"Mad" Anthony Wayne 1745-1796, Chester County. Revolutionary War general
John Weismuller 1904-1984, Windber. Five-time gold medal Olympic swimmer
Owen Wister 1860-1938, Philadelphia. Novelist: *The Virginian*
William Wrigley, Jr. 1861-1932, Philadelphia. Founder of Wrigley chewing gum company
Robert Yerkes 1876-1956, Breadysville. Psychologist

Colleges and Universities
There are many colleges and universities in Pennsylvania. Here are the more prominent, with their locations, dates of founding, and enrollment.

Albright College, Reading, 1856, 1,260
Allegheny College, Meadville, 1815, 1,783
Beaver College, Glenside, 1853, 1,175
Bloomsburg University of Pennsylvania, Bloomsburg, 1839, 6,978
Bryn Mawr College, Bryn Mawr, 1880, 1,208
Bucknell University, Lewisburg, 1846, 3,310
California University of Pennsylvania, California, 1852, 5,576
Carnegie-Mellon University, Pittsburgh, 1900, 4,302
Cedar Crest College, Allentown, 1867, 1,342
Chatham College, Pittsburgh, 1869, 630
Chestnut Hill College, Philadelphia, 1871, 911
Cheyney University of Pennsylvania, Cheyney, 1837, 1,262
Clarion University of Pennsylvania, Clarion, 1866, 5,691
Curtis Institute of Music,

Philadelphia, 1924, 125
Delaware Valley College of Science and Agriculture, Doylestown, 1896, 1,286
Dickinson College, Carlisle, 1773, 2,047
Drexel University, Philadelphia, 1891, 7,811
Duquesne University, Pittsburgh, 1878, 5,097
East Stroudsburg University of Pennsylvania, East Stroudsburg, 1893, 4,564
Edinboro University of Pennsylvania, Edinboro, 1859, 7,537
Elizabethtown College, Elizabethtown, 1899, 1,864
Franklin and Marshall College, Lancaster, 1787, 1800
Gannon University, Erie, 1933, 3,635
Geneva College, Beaver Falls, 1848, 1,380
Gettysburg College, Gettysburg, 1832, 1,950
Grove City College, Grove City, 1876, 2,217
Gwynedd-Mercy College, Gwynedd Valley, 1948, 1,474

Haverford College, Haverford, 1833, 1,138

Holy Family College, Philadelphia, 1954, 2,255

Immaculata College, Immaculata, 1920, 2,150

Indiana University of Pennsylvania, Indiana, 1875, 12,825

Juniata College, Huntingdon, 1876, 1,050

King's College, Wilkes-Barre, 1946, 2,312

Kutztown University of Pennsylvania, Kutztown, 1860, 6,784

Lafayette College, Easton, 1826, 2,225

La Salle University, Philadelphia, 1863, 4,751

Lebanon Valley College, Annville, 1866, 1,369

Lehigh University, Bethlehem, 1865, 4,473

Lock Haven University of Pennsylvania, Lock Haven, 1870, 3,878

Lycoming College, Williamsport, 1812, 1,478

Mansfield University of Pennsylvania, Mansfield, 1857, 2,915

Marywood College, Scranton, 1915, 1,858

Mercyhurst College, Erie, 1871, 2,259

Messiah College, Grantham, 1909, 2,263

Millersville University of Pennsylvania, Millersville, 1854, 6,125

Moore College of Art, Philadelphia, 1844, 450

Moravian College, Bethlehem, 1807, 1,174

Muhlenberg College, Allentown, 1848, 1,641

Penn State Erie, Behrend College, Erie, 1926, 2,975; *Harrisburg, Capital College,* Middletown, 1966, 2,314; *University Park Campus,* University Park, 1855, 31,805

Old main building at Penn State.

Philadelphia College of Bible, Langhorne, 1913, 779

Philadelphia College of Pharmacy and Science, Philadelphia, 1821, 1,654

Philadelphia College of Textiles and Science, Philadelphia, 1884, 2,780

Rosemont College, Rosemont, 1921, 600

Saint Francis College, Loretto, 1847, 1,136

Saint Joseph's University, Philadelphia, 1851, 3,804

Saint Vincent College, Latrobe, 1846, 1,248

Seton Hill College, Greensburg, 1883, 1,027

Shippensburg University of Pennsylvania, Shippensburg, 1871, 5,619

Slippery Rock University of Pennsylvania, Slippery

Rock, 1889, 7,024

Susquehanna University, Selinsgrove, 1858, 1,447

Swarthmore College, Swarthmore, 1864, 1,267

Temple University, Philadelphia, 1884, 27,736

Thiel College, Greenville, 1866, 897

University of Pennsylvania, Philadelphia, 1740, 22,418

University of Pittsburgh, Pittsburgh, 1787, 27,852; *at Bradford,* 1963, 1,309; *at Greensburg,* 1963, 1,465; *at Johnstown,* 1927, 3,243

University of Scranton, Scranton, 1888, 5,001

Ursinus College, Collegeville, 1869, 1,113

Villa Maria College, Erie, 1925, 638

Villanova University, Villanova,

1842, 11,413

Washington and Jefferson College, Washington, 1780, 1,144

Waynesburg College, Waynesburg, 1850, 1,351

West Chester University of Pennsylvania, West Chester, 1812, 11,806

Westminster College, New Wilmington, 1852, 1,554

Wilkes University, Wilkes-Barre, 1933, 3,200

Where To Get More Information

Pennsylvania Chamber of Commerce
222 N. 3rd Street
Harrisburg, PA 17101

or call, 1-800-VISITPA

Further Reading

General

Aylesworth, Thomas G., and Virginia L. *State Reports: Mid-Atlantic States.* New York: Chelsea House, Publishers, 1991.

Delaware

Carpenter, Allan. *Delaware,* rev. ed. Childrens Press, 1979.

Delaware: A Guide to the First State, rev. ed. (American Guide Series). Somerset, 1980.

Hoffecker, Carol E., ed. *Readings in Delaware History.* University of Delaware Press, 1974.

Kent, Deborah. *America the Beautiful: Delaware.* Chicago: Childrens Press, 1991.

Lyman, Nanci A. *The Colony of Delaware.* Watts, 1975.

Munroe, John A. *History of Delaware.* University of Delaware Press, 1979.

Maryland

Bode, Carl. *Maryland: A Bicentennial History.* Norton, 1978.

Carpenter, Allan. *Maryland,* rev. ed. Childrens Press, 1979.

Dozer, Donald M. *Portrait of a Free State: A History of Maryland.* Cornell Maritime Press, 1979.

Fradin, Dennis B. *The Maryland Colony.* Chicago: Childrens Press, 1990.

Kent, Deborah B. *America the Beautiful: Maryland.* Chicago: Childrens Press, 1991.

Papenfuse, Edward C., and others, eds. *Maryland: A New Guide to the Old Line State.* Johns Hopkins, 1976.

Pennsylvania

Baker, Bernadette, and Fran O'Byrne-Pelham. *Philadelphia.* Minneapolis: Dillon Press, 1989.

Carpenter, Allan. *Pennsylvania,* rev. ed. Childrens Press, 1979.

Cochrane, Thomas. *Pennsylvania: A Bicentennial History.* Norton, 1978.

Fradin, Dennis B. *The Pennsylvania Colony.* Chicago: Childrens Press, 1988.

Kent, Deborah B. *America the Beautiful: Pennsylvania.* Chicago: Childrens Press, 1988.

Lengyel, Emil. *The Colony of Pennsylvania.* Watts, 1974.

Numbers in italics refer to illustrations

Picture Credits

AP/Wide World Photos: pp. 24, 50, 51 (center), 85, 86, 87, 88; Courtesy of Delaware Office of Tourism: pp. 3 (top), 5, 7, 8-9, 11, 14, 15, 16, 19, 20, 22, 23 (top); Kevin Fleming: pp. 12, 13; Library of Congress: pp. 18, 46-47, 77, 80; Courtesy of Maryland Office of Tourism: pp. 3 (bottom), 26, 28-29, 31, 32, 33, 34, 36, 37, 38, 40, 43, 44, 45; Maryland State Archives: p. 25; National Graphic Center: p. 76; National Portrait Gallery, Smithsonian Institution: pp. 23 (bottom), 51 (left, right), 74, 81, 83; New York Public Library/Stokes Collection: p. 75; Pennsylvania Department of State: p. 53; Courtesy of Pennsylvania Office of Tourism: pp. 4, 54, 55, 56-57, 59, 60, 62, 63, 64, 66, 68, 69, 70, 71, 72-73, 78, 79, 82.

Cover photos courtesy of Delaware Office of Tourism; Maryland Office of Tourism; and Pennsylvania Office of Tourism.